Praise for *System*

T0344008

Harris and Jones deftly weave together seemingly polar opposite notions in education—equity and excellence—and provide persuasive arguments that the two are interrelated. *System Recall* proposes innovative and workable solutions to ensure that equity issues constitute the centerpiece of professional collaboration, policy-making, and educational reform. The key message is clear: poverty need not determine a child's life chances, choices, or destiny if schools provide interventions that mitigate the impact of poverty and inequity on educational outcomes.

—**Avis Glaze**, International Education Advisor,
British Columbia, Canada

This important book looks systemic inequity in the face and calls out those things that exacerbate educational disadvantage around the world: punitive accountability regimes, marketplace competition, and a hyper-focus on international large-scale testing. *System Recall* presents a simple premise: that equity leads to excellence. It calls for those leading schools and education systems to consider culture and context, and provides a clear set of guiding principles.

—**Deb Netolicky, Jon Andres**, and **Cameron Paterson**;
Editors of *Flip the System Australia*

In a time where "education has become the most important global currency," this book is both needed and timely. Only if we make the changes described in this book can we ensure high quality and equitable education for all of our students. This is what excellence looks like.

—**Kim Schildkamp**, University of Twente/ ICSEI president

System Recall: Leading for Equity and Excellence reminds all of us who are fortunate enough to be in leadership positions that achieving true excellence is only possible by placing ultimate value on equity.

—**Huw Foster Evans**, Chief Executive, National Academy for
Educational Leadership, Wales

Corwin Impact Leadership Series

Series Editor: Peter M. DeWitt

System Recall

Leading for Equity and Excellence in Education

Alma Harris

Michelle S. Jones

Forewords by

Adrian Piccoli and Yong Zhao

Corwin Impact Leadership Series

Series Editor: Peter M. DeWitt

FOR INFORMATION:

Corwin
A SAGE Company
2455 Teller Road
Thousand Oaks, California 91320
(800) 233-9936

www.corwin.com
SAGE Publications Ltd.
1 Oliver's Yard
55 City Road
London EC1Y 1SP
United Kingdom

SAGE Publications India Pvt. Ltd.
B 1/I 1 Mohan Cooperative Industrial Area
Mathura Road, New Delhi 110 044
India

SAGE Publications Asia-Pacific Pte. Ltd.
18 Cross Street #10-10/11/12
China Square Central
Singapore 048423

Publisher: Arnis Burvikovs
Development Editor: Desirée A. Bartlett
Senior Editorial Assistant: Eliza B. Erickson
Project Editor: Amy Schroller
Copy Editor: Erin Livingston
Typesetter: C&M Digitals (P) Ltd.
Proofreader: Talia Greenberg
Indexer: Sylvia Coates
Cover Designer: Candice Harman
Graphic Designer: Anupama Krishnan
Marketing Manager: Sharon Pendergast

Printed in the United States of America

ISBN 978-1-5443-4226-9

This book is printed on acid-free paper.

19 20 21 22 23 10 9 8 7 6 5 4 3 2 1

DISCLAIMER: This book may direct you to access third-party content via web links, QR codes, or other scannable technologies, which are provided for your reference by the author(s). Corwin makes no guarantee that such third-party content will be available for your use and encourages you to review the terms and conditions of such third-party content. Corwin takes no responsibility and assumes no liability for your use of any third-party content, nor does Corwin approve, sponsor, endorse, verify, or certify such third-party content.

Contents

Foreword

By *Adrian Piccoli*

Recent elections and numerous reports have highlighted the social tensions that arise when growing inequity marginalizes certain sectors of our society. With modern society at an increasing risk of splintering across economic, political, and geographic divides, the role that education will play in influencing this phenomenon sits at a crucial crossroad.

Pursuing school improvement through the status quo drivers of choice and competition is still defended by strong economic, cultural, and political forces. This no-change option stands to further entrench inequity through the segregation of students and community across class, wealth, and geography.

The alternative requires a total "system recall," as Alma Harris and Michelle Jones elegantly argue in *System Recall: Leading for Equity and Excellence in Education*. Their case for a fundamental change in the way education is viewed by the broader community and led by educators will not just affect students but will play a crucial role in underpinning our future cultural, social, and economic direction.

Harris and Jones lay out a comprehensive plan for education leaders at both a macro and micro level to create and foster equity as the path to better performance for all students. They do this by taking the reader through the research and the lived experiences of education leaders on how to drive education excellence by creating greater equity within systems and greater equity within schools.

From how to lead professional collaborations to leading parents and community engagement, this book provides a no-nonsense, practical guide to achieving school and student excellence through improving equity.

As Harris and Jones rightly say, equity matters—not just because it is the right of every child to reach their full potential, but for the future of our society itself.

—Professor Adrian Piccoli, Director
Gonski Institute for Education, School of Education
Faculty of Arts and Social Sciences
University of New South Wales
Sydney

Foreword

By Yong Zhao

"Education, then, beyond all other devices of human origin, is the great equalizer of the conditions of men—the balance-wheel of the social machinery" (Mann, 1848). These words of the father of American public education, Horace Mann, over 170 years ago epitomize the trust many hold in the power of education to lift people out of poverty, to remove the barriers to prosperity imposed by the conditions one is born into, and to create a more equal, peaceful, and cohesive society. But this trust can be and has been betrayed because the equalizing power of education is conditioned on how it is realized. When done right, education can indeed be the great equalizer Mann envisioned. But it can also exacerbate and perpetuate inequities and inequalities.

Alma Harris and Michelle Jones brilliantly make the case that "education systems in many countries currently contribute to the inequity problem" in this book. They present compelling evidence to show that "education systems are part of the inequity problem and many are persistently failing to address the needs of all learners." That is, instead of being the great equalizer, education, as practiced in many parts of the world today, works to reinforce the effect of inequalities into which children are born. Many education systems have built in or inherited features that reward and take care of the advantaged while neglect at the best and punish at the worst the disadvantaged children.

The problem of inequity in education has worsened in recent decades, despite and perhaps even because of efforts to address the issue of inequality, to close the "achievement gap," and to help children from disadvantaged backgrounds to perform as well as their advantaged peers (Zhao, 2016, 2018). These efforts, as Harris and Jones insightfully point out, are often rooted in the tradition of rewarding "excellence and performativity often in very narrow and selective ways." The so-called excellence is generally measured as test scores in a few school subjects and consequently equity is indicated by the gaps in test scores among different groups of students. As such, education systems and schools have become prisoners of international and national testing agencies, investing in policies and practices to raise their test scores.

These policies and practices are quite often based on a simplistic understanding of the causes and impact of poverty and other social inequalities on children as well as misinformed views of what makes good education for all children. Harris and Jones unapologetically and expertly expose the fundamental flaws of the ineffective and possibly harmful policies and practices promoted by international organizations such as PISA and national governments. "The hard truths" about inequity and inequality in education this book brings into the open not only explain why some policies and practices are ineffective and harmful to disadvantaged students but also shed light on what could work.

What could work to make education the great equalizer is at the heart of the book. Unlike many writings that stop at exposing the problems, which in and of itself is of course valuable, Harris and Jones suggest solutions. The two globally recognized leading thinkers with deep and broad experiences and expertise as teachers, leaders, and scholars present a series of actionable recommendations for policy makers and education leaders. These recommendations, drawn upon sound research and personal observations from around the world, are both macro and micro. They can have significant impact on addressing the problem of inequity and inequality in education.

The recommendations suggested by Harris and Jones can be challenging to follow because they ask for the removal of deeply entrenched features of education systems such as the obsession with testing and international rankings, the infatuation with "excellence", the delusion of borrowing from "top performers" to succeed, and the habit of blaming the victims—students, teachers, and school leaders. This is not to say that the recommendations are not practical. Quite on the contrary, as evidenced by the numerous examples included in this book, these recommendations have been practiced in many education systems around the world, albeit often in isolated contexts. What is needed is to expand and extend the impact of the recommended policies and practices into more schools and systems.

And this requires recognition and acceptance of the fact that the current systems in many countries are inadequate, defective, and inequitable. They need to be recalled. They need to be redesigned. They need to be redesigned to focus on equity because inequity in education cannot be allowed to continue. It is one of the greatest dangers facing humanity. "It is a risk to economic prosperity, a barrier to social cohesion and most importantly, a human tragedy."

To what extent education can truly become the great equalizer that Mann imagined depends on the actions of us, the collective of policy makers, parents, leaders, teachers, and children. *System Recall: Leading for Equity and Excellence in Education* provides an excellent guide for meaningful and impactful actions to make education more equitable.

—Yong Zhao
University of Kansas

Acknowledgments

This book would not have been possible without the enthusiasm and support of the Corwin team, particularly Arnis Burvikovs, Peter Dewitt, and Eliza Erickson. As part of the *Corwin Impact Leadership Series*, we are both honored and humbled to be part of such an impressive lineup of authors and titles.

This book contends that educational success should not be a matter of luck or chance or fate but rather is a fundamental entitlement for *all* students in *all* settings (Harris, 2008). We readily acknowledge that there are powerful barriers that continue to prevail and persist. We know that despite even the best efforts, some children are consistently left behind academically and left out socially. These are the brutal facts.

This book argues, however, that teachers, principals, communities, parents, and a whole host of organizations are leading for equity and excellence, relentlessly and effectively. There are many green shoots of success and many committed people working together, locally and nationally, to make a difference to the most vulnerable, needy, invisible, or forgotten children. This book proposes that their amazing work would be far more powerful and impactful if equity was at the real heart of policy making.

Hence, this is our plea for a "system recall" that recalibrates policy attention to equity first and excellence second.

Our heartfelt thanks go to the many wonderful research, policy, and practitioner colleagues around the world who support our work and contribute to our thinking: You know who you are, and we remain eternally in your debt.

To our families, who keep us grounded and loved: Thank you.

Lastly, to the future generations who grow up in a world where success for *all* students in *all* settings is the norm and not some distant aspiration: Thank you for continuing to ensure that equity and excellence are at the forefront of educational policy and practice.

About the Authors

Alma Harris (FAcSS, FLSW, FRSA) has held professorial posts at the University of Warwick, University College London, the University of Malaya, the University of Bath, and the University of Swansea. She is internationally known for her research and writing on educational leadership, education policy, and school improvement. In 2009–2012, she was a senior policy adviser to the Welsh government, assisting with the process of systemwide reform. She co-led the national professional learning communities (PLC) program and led on the development and implementation of a master's qualification for all newly qualified teachers in Wales. Since 2009, she has worked for the World Bank, contributing to development and research programs aimed at supporting schools in challenging contexts in Russia. Dr. Harris is a visiting professor at the Moscow Higher School of Economics and the University of Southampton. She is a Senior Research Fellow at the Education University of Hong Kong. Dr. Harris is past president of the International Congress for School Effectiveness and School Improvement (ICSEI), which is an organization dedicated to enhancing quality and equity in education. In January 2016, she received the ICSEI honorary lifetime award. In 2016, she was appointed to the International Council of Education Advisers (ICEA) to offer policy advice to Scotland's First Minister and Deputy First Minister. She is a Fellow of the Academy of Social Sciences, a Fellow of the Learned Society of Wales, and a Fellow of the Royal Society of Arts. Her website can be found at http://almaharris.com.

Michelle S. Jones is currently Head of Swansea University School of Education and Associate Professor of Leadership and Professional

Learning. She has previously held academic positions at the University of Bath, UK and the University of Malaya where she was the Deputy Director of the Institute of Educational Leadership.

Dr Jones' commitment to educational excellence has driven her entire career. She has worked with government agencies in England, Russia, Singapore, Australia, and Malaysia assisting with the design and delivery of their leadership and professional learning programs. Most recently, Dr Jones has been assisting the Welsh government in her role as Chair of the Professional Learning Accreditation Group for Wales: a national body comprising all universities working collaboratively to produce a National MA in Education. She previously was a professional adviser to the Welsh government and led a national program of professional learning for all schools in Wales.

Dr Jones has worked for the World Bank to develop a range of professional learning programs for teachers working in high-poverty schools in various countries. Her writing and research on professional learning communities is internationally known and she recently co-led a research project, funded by the Head Foundation, that focused on turnaround schools in Malaysia and Indonesia. Dr Jones has worked in many international research teams and is currently co-leading an ERASMUS project.

Dr Jones has considerable international expertise and experience. She is a Research Fellow of the Hong Kong Institute of Education and a Senior Research Fellow at the National Research University, Moscow Higher School of Economics. She is the co-editor of a well-established international journal "School Leadership and Management" that publishes articles, reports, news, and information on all aspects of the organization and management of schools and colleges.

Dr Jones is passionate about putting children first in all circumstances. Her research and development work continues to practically address the challenges of educational inequality and inequity. Dr Jones is a Fellow of the Royal Society of Arts.

Introduction

Ending educational inequality is going to require systemic change and a long-term, sustained effort.

Wendy Kopp (2012)

The world is changing and changing fast. The digital revolution is calling into question what we know and how we know it. Education has become the most important global currency, and evaluating information will be the most valuable life skill in the future. In times of great challenge or dynamic change, educators are advised to move toward the danger instead of retreating to a safer, more secure place (Fullan, 2003). This book argues that we now need to move toward the most potent and pervasive danger that negatively affects the lives and life chances of so many young people. That danger is inequity.

Inequity is one of the greatest challenges facing most education systems today. It is a risk to economic prosperity, a barrier to social cohesion, and, most importantly, a human tragedy. There is ample evidence that social factors, including education, employment status, income level, gender, and ethnicity, have a marked influence on physical and mental health. In all countries—whether low-, middle-, or high-income—there are wide disparities in the health status of different social groups. The lower an individual's socioeconomic position, the higher the risk of poor health (World Health Organization, 2017).

Health, income, and social differences are interrelated and combine, for some groups in society, into a powerful inequity mix. Such inequities have significant costs both to individuals and families. Inequity is also the root cause of many educational challenges globally, but in many of the contemporary debates about education, it often takes a back seat.

Conversations turn far more readily to failing schools (Weale, 2018a), poor teachers (Burns, 2012), or misbehaving children (Green, 2019), and solutions are sought to fix the parts of the system that seem to be most troublesome. Inequity, the major fault line between educational success and failure, is often ignored or sidelined in discussions about school and system performance. The main contributor to educational underachievement is neatly sidestepped in favor of more technical–rational solutions, usually in the shape of new initiatives, projects, or interventions.

Some of the interventions that aim to tackle the "deficits" in young people themselves are of most concern. For example, research published by the Education Endowment Foundation (EEF) charity in the UK found that programs aimed at changing the way schoolchildren think about themselves and their intelligence (i.e., changing mindsets) need to be in-depth and sustained in order to make a measurable difference to their school results (Rolfe, 2015).

Pupils whose teachers received the mindset training made no additional progress compared to those in control group schools, although they did show a better understanding of the malleability of intelligence. This was measured by their understanding of three statements written by Carol Dweck (2015), such as, "You have a certain amount of intelligence and you really can't do much to change it." This is worrying in many respects, most of all because it positions blame on individuals and away from the prime causes of underachievement that are societal and systemic.

The fact remains that growing up poor affects millions of young people worldwide. Poverty is a global issue, and closing the attainment gap between the rich and the poor remains a significant and persistent challenge. Poverty, and the multiple disadvantages that accompany it, is the most pressing economic, societal, and educational issue. As Figure 0.1 below shows, persistent poverty in some regions (and growing inequalities worldwide) are stark reminders that economic globalization and liberalization have not

Figure 0.1 Global and Regional Trends in Extreme Poverty, 1981–2005

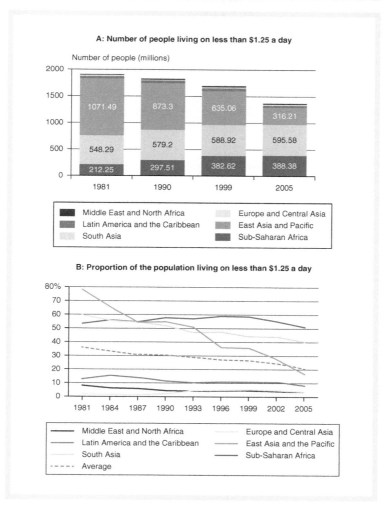

Source: Based on data from World Bank Development Research Group (2009). See also UNDESA (2010).

created an environment conducive to sustainable and equitable social development.

If education is a fundamental human right, then why do so many young people living in poverty have substandard or unequal experiences of schooling in the 21st century? Why does poverty continue to be the prime determinant of educational failure? This book argues that equitable education is a fundamental human right that can be achieved only through major structural change and making choices about what matters most in education.

Right now in the world's richest countries, some children achieve less than others at school simply because of circumstances far beyond their control. Where they were born, the languages they speak, their ethnicity, their race, or their parents' occupation can be significant barriers to educational opportunity and inclusion. These children enter schooling already at a significant disadvantage and can drop further behind if educational policies and practices reinforce rather than reduce the gap between them and their peers (United Nations Children's Fund [UNICEF], 2018).

Not all children reach their full potential to pursue their interests or to develop their talents and skills. This has huge personal, social, economic, and human costs. Most of the children who fall through the educational net live in acute poverty and deprivation. While disadvantage is not an excuse for low achievement and attainment, it certainly continues to be a potent explanatory factor.

This book argues that the negative relationship between disadvantage and educational achievement can be weakened, but only if the structural features that perpetuate and reproduce educational winners and losers are fully addressed. In industry, if a product is faulty in any way, it is recalled; it is removed from sale; it is discontinued.

This book proposes that a "system recall" is needed in education, as many education systems are part of the inequity problem. Many are persistently failing to address the needs of all learners. In short, this book proposes that there needs to be a radical rethinking of *who* and *what* is most important in education. While the rhetoric and countless interventions to close the equity gap are laudable, they line up against deep, structural inequities that are potent and persistent.

THE ARGUMENT

The argument in this book is twofold. Firstly, it proposes that education systems in many countries currently contribute to the inequity problem because they continue to reward excellence and performativity in very narrow and selective ways, which leads to feelings of alienation on the part of teachers, and students. This is further exacerbated by the fact that contradictory signals are sent out by education policy makers about what's most important. One day it's tackling poverty, the next day it is reducing the attainment gap, the next it is addressing students' mental health and well-being. Yet what they incentivize, reward, and celebrate signals very clearly that these goals are not what they value most.

Education systems value high performance and high standards. This is not surprising at all, but too often, equality and equity appear to be second-order considerations. This book argues that excellence is the outcome of equity and that equitable education systems offer a route to better performance for all students.

Secondly, this book proposes that while education systems are the right unit of change for securing and sustaining equitable educational processes and outcomes, every day in schools, educators tackle some of the worse aspects or features of inequality and inequity.

This book takes a long, hard, and uncomfortable look at why equity is a laudable goal for so many educationalists and policy makers but is not likely to be achieved or sustained without significant structural reform. The book considers some of the structural features that are potent barriers to social justice; these are the hard truths. The book also focuses on the micro strategies and approaches that educators are adopting to turn around the fortunes of young people from the poorest communities and to reduce inequities wherever possible.

The aim of the book is to prompt reflection and discussion about educational equity and excellence by drawing upon a wide range of international evidence, including the research work of the authors over many years. Both of us have taught in schools serving highly deprived communities and have led, in various capacities, within schools located in areas of high poverty. Our research and writing focus on improving schools and school systems in various countries.

We remain committed to challenging inequity and inequality in education systems wherever and whenever they appear. Our writing, research, and developmental work with teachers and school leaders over more than three decades are reflected in the pages that follow.

There is no one strategy or approach that will work universally to fix the equity gap. To quote a rather overused phrase, there is no silver bullet. This book argues that both macro and micro approaches to change are needed to recalibrate education systems toward equity and excellence. Macro issues and hard truths are examined in Chapter 3. The micro, school-level approaches that reduce inequities are outlined in Chapters 4, 5, and 6.

Collectively, these chapters suggest that it is possible to overcome some of the barriers facing young people from disadvantaged backgrounds or marginalized circumstances. None of this, however, happens without effective leadership at all levels. Leadership remains the most potent lever in any change or improvement process; consequently, leading for equity and excellence requires principled and moral leadership throughout the system.

If educational equity and excellence is to be more than merely a policy strap-line, a distant aspiration, or the latest educational slogan, then it is imperative to understand where the real pitfalls lie and where genuine potential exists to reduce inequities. This book examines the *real* rather than *perceived* barriers to educational inequity at the macro level while also considering the micro practices that promote greater inclusion, student engagement, and raised attainment. This book proposes that excellence is achieved *through* equity[1] rather than despite it.

In the pages that follow, a case is made to realign education systems more closely to the needs of *all* young people (not just *some*) and to move away from large-scale international assessments and toward smaller data sets that are contextually appropriate and illuminate specific learner needs (Sharratt, 2018). If education is a right for all, irrespective of background or circumstance, then a major structural shift is required to reposition equity at the epicenter of education policy and practice.

---

[1]The phrase *excellence through equity* is attributed to Professor Andy Hargreaves.

CHAPTER

1

Inequality and Inequity

An imbalance between rich and poor is the oldest and most fatal ailment of all republics.

Plutarch, 46–120 CE

Inequality in education is not a new phenomenon. It is well established that unequal societies create damage not only to the poorest in society but to the whole population. Ichiro Kawachi (n.d.), a professor of social epidemiology at Harvard, has called inequality "a social pollutant" that affects mental health, physical well-being, and educational opportunities. His research work focuses on the negative effects of inequality on the health of certain groups and individual stress levels. His work highlights the detrimental effects of poverty on health and well-being, with the associated implications for unequal educational progress.

In 2018, a report on the state of education in England (Polianskaya, 2018) concluded that education reforms were causing greater inequality, with fewer children from less-well-off backgrounds attending higher-rated schools. The authors found that the education system in England was growing more inequitable:

> At present we see a system of winners and losers, with increasing incoherence and a loss of equity as a result. While higher status schools seemed to be benefiting from [education] policies, schools on the other end of the spectrum were facing more challenges, the study found, such as being undersubscribed and having "disproportionate numbers of disadvantaged, migrant and hard-to-place children."

Tackling inequity means addressing its bedfellow, *inequality*. Inequity and inequality are distinctive but potent influences that negatively affect levels of educational achievement and attainment. Global Health Europe (2009) explains the distinction:

> Inequity and inequality: these terms are sometimes confused, but are not interchangeable, inequity refers to unfair, avoidable differences arising from poor governance, corruption or cultural exclusion while inequality simply refers to the uneven distribution of health or health resources as a result of genetic or other factors or the lack of resources.

Social inequities are essentially disparities in power and wealth, often accompanied by discrimination or social exclusion. Inequity is a lack of justice, a sense of deep unfairness that goes beyond unequal resourcing and falls into discrimination, prejudice, or the exclusion of certain (often minority) groups. Sometimes inequities can lead to—and can cause—inequalities. Inequality and inequity are powerfully related and intertwined.

In 1948, the Universal Declaration of Human Rights listed free quality primary education as a right. The 1960 United Nations Educational, Scientific, and Cultural Organization (UNESCO) Convention Against Discrimination in Education reinforced the right to a quality primary education. The Convention on the Rights of the Child states that all children should have equal access to a quality education. The Convention stipulates that children should receive an education that allows them to be the best they can be so they can reach their full potential. The United Nations Millennium Development Goals reinforce free universal primary education as a right.

The Sustainability Development Goals 2015–2030 (Goal 2, n.d.) state that the most important priorities are to

1. end poverty in all its forms everywhere;
2. end hunger, achieve food security and improved nutrition, and promote sustainable agriculture;
3. ensure healthy lives and promote well-being for all at all ages;
4. ensure inclusive and equitable quality education and promote lifelong learning opportunities for all; and
5. achieve gender equality and empower all women and girls.

Despite all these important declarations and intentions, there are still children around the world who do not receive a free primary education. There are still schools that are not adequately resourced in both developed and developing countries. There are still schools in which children are learning in makeshift structures or buildings that are dangerous or unfit for this purpose. There are still classrooms that don't have a teacher and there are still children not able to go to school because of family circumstances. In summary, in the 21st century, inequality remains a prevalent and persistent block to the educational success of the poorest children in the poorest countries.

Tackling inequality in education therefore is fundamentally concerned with addressing unequal access to high-quality education in the shape of better schools and a critical imbalance in the allocation of educational resources. This unequal playing field can be leveled, but only through the redistribution of wealth and the specific targeting of extra resources to select groups of students.

Many education systems are actively trying to tackle inequalities through a process of resource redistribution that is fairer and more equal to all. Essentially, there are policy imperatives in place to ensure that more resources follow young people who are most in need. For example, the Scottish government has allocated £120 million to Pupil Equity Funding to tackle this attainment gap (https://www.gov.scot/policies/schools/pupil-attainment/).

Research undertaken by the Sutton Trust (Jerrim, 2017) found that 15-year-olds from poorer families in Scotland were found to be roughly 2–3 years behind their better-off peers in science, math, and reading. Consequently, Pupil Equity Funding is being provided as part of the £750 million Attainment Challenge Fund allocated to tackle the underachievement resulting from poverty. Pupil Equity Funding is allocated directly to schools and targeted at closing the poverty-related attainment gap.

Every council area in Scotland benefits from Pupil Equity Funding, and 95% of schools in Scotland have been allocated funding for pupils known to be eligible for free school meals. Funding is spent at the discretion of the head teacher working in partnership with others and the local authority. There is evidence (Scottish Government, 2018) that local authorities are using the additional money they receive as part of the Attainment Challenge to focus much more specifically on resourcing and supporting young people who are most in need.

The poverty-related attainment gap is common in many other developed countries. For example, in Australia, the high-profile Gonski Review (Parliament of Australia, n.d.) identified gaps in the educational outcomes of poorer Australian students. The review found that over the past decade, the performance of Australian students had declined at all levels of achievement outlined in international benchmarks. Furthermore, a significant proportion of Australia's lowest-performing students were found not to be meeting minimum standards of achievement. In short, the review found that Australia has a significant gap between its highest- and lowest-performing students, far greater than in many Organization for Economic Cooperation and Development (OECD) countries.

Gonski underlined the need for a more equitable school funding system, one that ensures that differences in educational outcomes are not the result of differences in wealth, income, power, or possessions. To address the current imbalances, it recommended a national needs-based and sector-blind school funding model.

The impact of this extra resource has been significant. Two principals explain the importance of extra funding.

Lithgow High School is a comprehensive high school with a concentration of disadvantaged students (more than 80% in the bottom two quartiles). It strives to provide outstanding "opportunities for everyone."

In 2014, the school received needs-based funding of 1.3 million dollars. The funding has been used to create access to resources for students that their more-privileged peers have been provided with by their parents/families. These include access to large software programs such as Mathletics, ClickView, Wheelers online library, Accelerated Reader, and online tuition for senior students. The latter was accessed voluntarily more than 11,029 times by students in 2018. In addition, there is a comprehensive wraparound well-being framework, including an onsite well-being center that provides students with access to specialist support services. In 2018, more than 800 sessions were delivered.

The impact of this extra resource has contributed to the creation of a positive and caring culture and growing motivation and confidence in students so that they can be successful. There has also been a positive impact on achievement in the Higher School Certificate (HSC) bands and a parallel drop in Band 3 results of 50%. Students receiving first-round university offers have increased by more than 50% in 2018.

Ann Caro
Principal
Lithgow High School

Merrylands East Public School is located in the southwestern part of Sydney and serves a culturally diverse community of 370 students from 40 different language backgrounds. About 10%

(Continued)

(Continued)

of students have refugee experiences (mainly from Afghanistan, Iran, and Iraq), and 60 students have been identified as having a disability.

Merrylands East Public School uses the flexible Gonski funding to address the literacy and numeracy needs of students by engaging a specialist and former high school math teacher to assist Stage 3 (Years 5 and 6) students and specialist early intervention literacy teachers with programs such as Reading Recovery, Early Action for Success, and Play-Based Learning.

While Merrylands East does not focus on National Assessment Program—Literacy and Numeracy (NAPLAN), the school has consistently been acknowledged by the Australian Curriculum and Reporting Authority (ACARA) as achieving high growth and added value for their students.

John Goh
@johnqgoh
Principal/Primary Principals Forum Spokesperson
Merrylands East Public School

These school examples underline the importance of extra resources (carefully spent) in maximizing learning for students who are at a disadvantage in order to raise aspirations and attainment for all. As highlighted earlier, inequality and inequity are difficult to tackle, and while extra resources are critically important, this remains only part of all the solution.

INEQUITY

Inequality, like inequity, is hardwired into the DNA of many countries and is reflected and reinforced in their education systems. Inequity is notoriously difficult to disturb or disrupt. As Chapter 3 outlines, the hard truths about structural barriers make inequity difficult to uproot. Challenging inequity, therefore, requires more than the reallocation or redistribution of resources. It necessitates dismantling the structural barriers that serve to exacerbate and perpetuate inequity.

This does not mean, or indeed suggest, that educators are not doing their best to tackle inequity wherever they find it. The reverse is true. Rather, it is to propose that all those efforts would be far more effective and impactful within an education system that was premised firmly upon equity in the first place.

In Finland, enhancing equity has been the driving principle in its education system since the 1970s (Sahlberg, 2018). While Finland has become the automatic go-to example of everything that seems good in education, long before the arrival of the Program for International Student Assessment (PISA), the Finnish education system reflected both excellence and equity. UNESCO global education monitoring report data show that in Finland, the attainment gap between rich and poor is marginal. In addition, 0% of the population in Finland earn less than 1.9 dollars a day. As the Finnish educator Pasi Sahlberg (2018) outlines, "Finland cannot afford to leave any child behind. We know from our own statistics that more equitable education is also cost-beneficial in the long run" (p. 54).

Finland does not engage in competition, merit-based pay, or privatization—features so predominantly displayed in the educational landscape of many other systems within developed and developing countries. Finnish schools serve all children equally. A high-performing school in Finland is one where all students perform beyond expectations, which may mean different things for different students. The education system in Finland reflects certain societal norms and democratic values that support and value educational equity.

In the Netherlands (Jones et al., 2017), there also exists a strong cultural disposition toward equity, reflected throughout its society and its educational system. There is strong local control of education, and municipalities enact democratic decision making. In many ways, the Netherlands is an example of educational equity and excellence, even though it has far less press exposure than Finland. Like Finland, however, not one of its 17.1 million population earns less than 1.9 dollars an hour.

Canada offers another strong example of equity and excellence. Learners in Canada are far ahead of their geographic neighbors in the United States in terms of equity and excellence. Canada has the world's highest proportion of working-age adults who have been through higher education—55%, compared with an average of 35% in OECD countries. Canada also has a high level of migrants in its school population.

More than a third of young adults in Canada are from families where their parents are from another country. Yet the children of newly arrived, migrant families seem to integrate rapidly enough to perform at the same high level as their classmates. The equity gap in Canada is far narrower than in most other developed countries. Despite the different policies in individual provinces, there is a common commitment to an equal chance in school, which makes Canada (like Finland) a system that invests in equity in order to achieve excellence.

In summary, it is not *one thing* that explains the equitable approach of the Netherlands, Canada, or Finland; it's a *system thing*. The entire system in each of these countries is premised upon equity. Other countries interested in better performance might be advised to think about how far their system is equitable and whether this is most important.

WHAT IS MOST IMPORTANT?

Children have one chance to flourish, to develop their talents, and to realize their true potential. There are no second chances, no reruns, no repeats. If inequity exists in any system, then it disenfranchises and deliberately excludes some young people and not others. The net result is the reinforcement that some children are expected to succeed and others are routinely expected to fail.

Yet, for many children, the odds are steadily stacked against them because of the powerful forces of disadvantage that are beyond their control. These forces result in major differences in the access to and the quality of the education that these young people receive. In this way, inequity is an invasive part of their educational experience, operating in punitive and powerful ways.

Not only are certain young people valued in some education systems far more than others but they are also rewarded differently. Apart from the inherent moral and ethical considerations, the social and economic consequences are also stark, as countless young people are destined to be educationally, economically, and socially abandoned.

The performance gap between the richest and the poorest has remained persistently large between the mid-1980s and the mid-2000s, with no significant improvement. Comparing the performance of 11-year-olds born in 2000 with those born in 1970 reveals that the geographic area a child comes from has become a more powerful predictive factor for those born in 2000 compared to 1970 (Clegg, Allen, Fernandes, Freedman, & Kinnock, 2017, p. 6).

A recent OECD (2018) report notes that no country in the world can claim that it has totally eradicated all forms of inequality and inequity, not even Finland. There is no educational system that can claim that, either. The forces of poverty and disadvantage, however small, still work against a fair, just, and equal experience of schooling. Overlay this with the impact of race, gender, class, and socioeconomic status differences, and the possibility of equitable education seems like a distant dream.

The main messages from research are crystal clear: Structural inequalities in society lead to unequal access and outcomes; therefore, recalibrating funding, resources, and action to support children in various levels of disadvantage is not only important but is imperative if social justice is the core aim. Young people who are disenfranchised and disconnected are often the most vulnerable in society and are in need of support, care, and nurturing within a supportive school and community environment. They do not need another punitive behavior policy (Roberts, 2019) or an intervention aimed at developing their resilience or grit to succeed (Bazelais et al., 2018). These young people are not the problem.

The wealth divide is growing, and with it, the gap between the educational attainment of those at the top and bottom of society. While there is a strong commitment from many governments to greater educational equality and equity, the evidence about social mobility would suggest that the stubborn patterns of inequity within societies prevail and persist (OECD, 2018).

Social and educational mobility are important because they reflect the equality of opportunity in society. Inequality and inequity mean wasted talent, sidelined human potential, and a failure of the most vulnerable young people in society.

It could be concluded that there is little that can be done, as so much has already been tried. Yet the international discourse is changing, and more questions are being asked about the contributors to inequality and inequity. The Economic Policy Institute (García & Weiss, 2017) in the United States concluded that

> extensive research has conclusively demonstrated that children's social class is one of the most significant predictors—if not the single most significant predictor—of their educational success. Moreover, it is increasingly apparent that performance gaps by social class take root in the earliest years of children's lives and fail to narrow in the years that follow. That is, children who start behind stay behind—they are rarely able to make up the lost ground.

This report concludes that such trends have critical implications for policy and for society. Failing to provide the foundational experiences and opportunities that all children need to succeed in school and thrive in life has serious implications that should be a matter of grave concern for policy makers.

TIME TO STOP AND THINK

These are uncertain and challenging times to be a young person, to be a teacher, to be a policy maker, to be a parent. One thing is clear, however: Excellence at the expense of equity is a dramatic waste of human potential. Token policies aimed at closing the gap are, by themselves, woefully insufficient to do the job. Failed policies often follow other failed policies.

While the policy machinery keeps turning and churning out new mandates for change, for those who teach and learn in schools, the pressure of change is relentless. Despite decades of reform, in many countries, there is still relatively little change in patterns of inequity (OECD, 2018). While pockets of success can be found, of course, these are rarely scaled up to a level in which a dramatic shift occurs throughout the system.

One of the reasons why inequity continues to have a powerful grip on educational outcomes is the fact that so many education systems are fixated with a narrow range of measurements, confusing these with the purposes and intentions of education. A report by Kirstin Kerr and Mel Ainscow called *Equity in Education: Time to Stop and Think* argues that it is difficult to "square demands for increased excellence understood in terms of narrow academic attainment with the realities of children's lives outside school" (Kerr & Ainscow, 2017, p. 5).

These authors propose that punitive accountability regimes and the vagaries of marketplace competition have fueled inequity in many countries. They conclude that "all this suggests that a more equitable education system cannot only be concerned with a narrowly defined set of standards. A broader vision of the purposes of education is needed to supplement this and to guide the system's development" (Kerr & Ainscow, 2017, p. 9).

Recalibrating the policy dial toward equity rather than excellence is not without its inherent challenges, but without a clear focus on "success for every child in every setting" (Harris, 2008), schools and school systems will continue to systematically deny certain young people their educational right.

EXCELLENCE EXPOSED

If you consider system performance from the perspective of equity rather than excellence, this calls into question any desire to emulate or borrow from some of the PISA high flyers. For example, Singapore does not include most special needs students in its mainstream classrooms. As one commentator notes,

Singaporeans support the idea of inclusion but do not walk the talk. . . . One possible reason why special needs children, such as those with learning and behavioural difficulties or physical disabilities, are not accepted fully in society is the lack of interaction between the public and such children. (Tai, 2016)

In China, there is a similar story. Children with disabilities face significant hurdles in accessing education, and a substantial number of them receive no education at all.

In higher education, government guidelines allow universities to restrict or bar access to applicants and students with certain physical or mental disabilities. There are at least 83 million people with disabilities in China, according to official statistics. Over 40 percent of them are illiterate. While government figures show near universal enrollment of children in primary school, there is a large gap for children with disabilities: 28 percent of such children are not receiving the basic education to which they are entitled. (Human Rights Watch, 2013)

In South Korea, children with intellectual and physical disabilities struggle at regular schools, where they often find themselves unsupervised.

Although most children with disabilities attend regular schools as part of the government's goal for an inclusive education system, their needs often go unnoticed or ignored. But even as parents try to find other options, these rarely exist. (Global Accessibility News, 2017)

Is this what other systems really want to replicate? Can excellence at the expense of equity ever be justifiable? Is excellence over equity the real reason for the continued poverty-related education gap? The next chapter takes a more detailed look.

CHAPTER
2

Excellence Over Equity?

Caring about and believing in young people is obviously fundamental to student success. Increasing the opportunity to learn is core to the equity effort in education.

Mica Pollock (2017)

In *Schooltalk*, Mica Pollock suggests that *equity* means supporting the full talent development of every student and all groups of students. In her view, equity within schools encompasses respecting all students, meeting a variety of student needs, and offering a wide range of learning opportunities. She advocates that the nature of our language and the way we communicate with students is a key contributor to reducing inequities in the classroom. What we say and how we say it can have a significant impact on young people who are marginalized, feel vulnerable, or are at risk. Taking care with language and communication is, as Pollock so ably argues, an important part of making *all* students feel valued.

Achieving equity in education is about providing equal opportunities to learn for all students. Providing equal opportunities means that "diligent attention has to be paid, at the macro and micro levels, to how society and schools can address unequal processes and outcomes" (Datnow & Park, 2019, p. 19). A global obsession with narrow definitions and measures of educational excellence, however, continues to overshadow inequity and inequality.

This chapter explores how inequities are generated and reinforced at the macro or system level. It proposes that inequities in the system are the direct result of certain structural features, policies, and processes within different education systems. As Yong Zhao (2019) argues, the *side effects* of many educational policies and reform processes harm the very people that they were intended to help. He explains,

> "This medicine can reduce fever, but it can cause a bleeding stomach." When you buy a medical product, you are given information about both its effects and side effects. But such practice does not exist in education. "This program helps improve your students' reading scores, but it may make them hate reading forever." No such information is given to teachers or school leaders. "This practice can help your children become a better student, but it may make her less creative." No parent has been given information about effects and side effects of practices in schools. "School choice may improve test scores of some students, but it can lead to the collapse of American public education." The public has not received information about the side effects of sweeping education policies.

The basic message here is that the intended effects of educational products, programs, policies, and practices are treated as if there are zero adverse effects. As Zhao (2019) warns, "The side effects exist the same way in education as in medicine." The clear implication is that studying and reporting the side effects of education policy and interventions is as important as studying and reporting the intended effects. All effects are important to consider when introducing or advocating any new policy, new intervention, or new stipulation.

Making a similar point, Viviane Robinson (2017) proposes that not all change is desirable and that it is important to distinguish between *change* and *improvement*. She argues,

> Instead of taking for granted that change will lead to improvement, we should do the opposite—that is, believe that change will not deliver our intended improvement unless there are structures and processes in place for ensuring that all involved can learn how to turn change into the intended improvement. (p. 5)

In Chapter 3, the hard truths of educational improvement and change are outlined. It suggests that there are critical fault lines (hard truths) that can have a profoundly negative effect on any attempt at tackling social injustices. Essentially, these fault lines contribute to (and in some cases, actively maintain) inequities and inequalities in education.

EXCELLENCE OVER EQUITY?

Around the globe, large-scale international assessments continue to define and measure what counts as educational excellence (Breakspear, 2016). In the United States, Sweden, and England, for example, more accountability-led school improvement processes have been introduced to rachet up educational performance (Shirley, 2017). Accountability measures often appear under the veneer of more palatable policy labels such as "narrowing the gap" or "no child left behind." These labels appear to speak to equity and equality, but the educational practices they encourage could not be further away.

Underneath such policy headlines often lurks a set of punitive accountability measures that are damaging the young people they say they are designed to help. Diane Ravitch (2000, 2016) has repeatedly noted how accountability, standardization, and testing regimes are used in ways that actively damage schools, students, and their communities. Charter schools are increasingly segregating students, leaving students from poorer communities excluded and their learning opportunities restricted. As one commentator proposed (Robinson, 2019),

> It's time to talk about "charter school privilege." That's the privilege that allows some of us to choose a charter school and to deny how that choice arises from an educational system characterized by racial, financial, and educational inequality and injustice. The groups, persons, and conditions that have made charter schools possible are also the groups, persons, and conditions that have weakened many traditional public schools, and exacerbated problems that further lead more parents to move their children to charters.

Furthermore, it has been argued that school choice is steadily eroding equal educational opportunities:

> Children are not exposed to the same educational opportunities. . . . Those in high-income families have a significantly easier time accessing high-quality education. Additionally, as intergenerational mobility has stalled, higher-income parents have become even more devoted to hoarding educational opportunities for their children. In a changing world with less social mobility, parents often believe that education will give their children [the] elusive tools necessary to advance in an increasingly competitive society. (Wingfield, 2019)

In Australia, the National Assessment Program—Literacy and Numeracy (NAPLAN) testing regime has been criticized because of similar concerns about the way in which these tests are used to sort pupils and to rank schools (Baker, 2019a). All students in Years 3, 5, 7, and 9 in Australia sit the NAPLAN, which is an ongoing part of Australia's National Assessment Program (NAP). NAPLAN is a national assessment that tests students' ability in three areas of literacy—reading, writing, and language conventions (spelling, grammar, and punctuation)—and in numeracy. Schools in all states and territories have administered NAPLAN in May every year since 2008.

Critics of NAPLAN suggest that it is divisive and that schools that receive good NAPLAN scores by default receive more attention from middle-class parents and are more able to move into the catchment area.

In some areas of Sydney, it has warped the public system, with parents flocking to schools with strong NAPLAN results and leaving those nearby (which might be better in other ways) half-empty (Baker, 2019b). Even supporters admit that the similar schools' measure is misleading, pitting selective schools against comprehensive ones and diverse schools against those with high English-speaking populations.

In addition, the intense pressure that is placed on schools to do well in tests is passed on to students; in many countries, this negatively affects their well-being and mental health (Weale, 2018b). The Grattan Institute in Australia undertook research that highlighted how far mental illness impacts upon a child's schooling. Their report notes that mental health issues have a bigger impact on young people's attainment than living in the bush or coming from a family where the parents/families didn't finish school.

Most significantly, the report found that mental illness had the biggest impact on students' numeracy performance, with Year 9 students lagging 21 months behind their mentally healthy peers. In reading, students with mental health issues were 18 months behind their Year 9 peers (Cook, 2019).

The relentless pursuit of high-stakes accountability in many systems has harmed schools, teachers, young people, and their communities. While the logic of standards and rigor seems appealing and persuasive, the question remains: At what cost?

While the tide in the United States and many other education systems is gradually turning to far greater consideration of students' well-being, mental health, and inclusion, it remains the case that in terms of education policy, excellence still overshadows equity. Even though many education systems espouse both excellence and equity, their policies and resulting actions continue to privilege and reinforce excellence *over* equity. Education ministers may say they want equity and excellence, but their policy orientations and actions show they simply want better Program for International Student Assessment (PISA) scores.

LEANING TOWER OF PISA

PISA is one of the main culprits in the ongoing attention imbalance between excellence and equity. PISA has become *the* measure—not *a* measure—of educational excellence internationally. Whether they concur or not, policy makers in various countries have become ardent followers of the Organization for Economic Cooperation and Development's version of educational excellence. Even if there is some acknowledgement that PISA has its limitations, like gamblers, policy makers return to the PISA table every 3 years, hoping for a different outcome.

The latest round of PISA testing took place in April 2018, and new rounds of PISA are already under preparation with new aspects to be included in addition to the core domains: reading, mathematics, and science. There is the introduction of "Baby PISA" testing for those under 5 years old and tests that are more culturally and contextually attuned. The Organization for Economic Cooperation and Development (OECD) version of educational excellence unquestionably has a tight grip globally. Some would argue that this global hold restricts a much-needed debate about the purposes and values of education (Netolicky, Andrews, & Paterson, 2018).

The logic of 21st-century skills espoused in the OECD's brand of educational excellence (Lauder et al., 2020) implies that the OECD is somehow more forward-looking and knowledgeable about the future needs of society than anyone else. Commercial companies have been quick to latch on to the OECD educational narrative and to take advantage of the profitable opportunities it brings.

In its press release on December 10, 2014, Pearson (2014) announced that it had won a competitive tender by the OECD to develop the Frameworks for PISA 2018. The main tasks were to

- redefine reading literacy, considering how young people are taught to approach the digital environment, including how to recognize credible websites and online documents;
- review and (where necessary) adapt the frameworks for mathematics and science;

- develop the student questionnaire framework for the collection of contextual information and the measurement of other education outcomes, which may have connections with performance;

- develop a framework for the measurement of global competence, which will assess students' awareness of the interconnected global world we live and work in and their ability to deal effectively with the resulting demands.

There are several issues here. Firstly, the task of defining global competence and then measuring it across diverse jurisdictions with any degree of precision is inherently problematic. Secondly, assessing global competency through a computer-based test has its risks. In 2019, New York State abandoned its computer-based testing process because of technical glitches in the system. Thirdly, allowing Pearson, a for-profit giant, to be the central designer and administrator of the tests must be a concern. Commercializing education, as Chapter 3 outlines, is part of the increased privatization of education, with all its consequences.

In the last decade or more, global policy agendas most evident in countries such as England and the United States have attempted to replace bureaucratic centralism with policies designed to deliver decentralized control, school choice, and market-based competition between schools. This neoliberalist or managerialist approach operates fundamentally on a market-based logic. One of the overriding concerns about the creation of quasi-markets in education is that by incentivizing competition between schools for resources, it effectively installs a private or business logic at the heart of a public system. PISA contributes to this business logic by pointing out, through its league tables, the shortcomings of entire education systems. This is an open door to private enterprises that are encouraged to walk in and, for a price, solve the problem.

Interestingly, many countries (including the United States and England) have already opted out of the PISA global competence test. Other countries, including Germany, France, Denmark, the Netherlands, Finland, and Ireland, have followed quickly, although they will take the other core academic subject tests. Inevitably, this raises some serious questions not only about the global competence test itself but also about how meaningful or valid comparisons can be made across the countries that remain (Coughlan, 2018).

Every few years, the global policy gaze turns to the comparison of countries based on PISA tests for a sample of 15-year-olds. PISA has become an educational beauty contest, but it also has its dark side. There are inevitable and, some would argue, predictable winners and losers.

For those at the top of the PISA tables, there is considerable international interest in following in their tracks. Many books, papers, reports, and articles offer explanations for better PISA performance, even though there is no certain way of knowing what will improve PISA scores. They remind us that in Finland, schools do "this" or that in Singapore, schools do "that" with a clear implication that whatever "this" or "that" may be, it must be good. The global appetite for learning the secret of PISA success and then copying it has created an entire PISA industry of predictions and practical advice.

While PISA has proffered the opportunity to compare the performance of different countries based on its data, it has also encouraged a penchant for borrowing from the best. While the Finnish educator, Pasi Sahlberg, strongly advises that others not copy Finland, this advice is often ignored in the international stampede for better system and school outcomes. Books offer "lessons" from the high performers, even though there is no possibility of empirically proving any direct cause and effect. Policies are borrowed from the best PISA performers out of context, based on little more than approximation, guesswork, or conjecture (Harris & Jones, 2018).

Since the first PISA results were published in December 2001, this international assessment has strengthened its grip on educational policy making globally and nationally. Although the impact of PISA may differ across national and even sub-national contexts, there are overarching elements identified within the literature as potential mechanisms behind PISA's ability to generate impact. One significant argument is that PISA employs mechanisms of *soft power* whereby the status of the OECD as an international organization allows for powerful yet indirect governance to influence policy making at the national level. Furthermore, it has been argued that

> the OECD's promotion of the use of PISA data upholds a desire for data-driven policy making at the national level, encouraging systems of weak governance relying upon external authorities such as the OECD for knowledge production and policy guidance. (Hopfenbeck et al., 2017, p. 14)

For this and many other reasons, it is worth looking at PISA in a little more depth.

PISA Uncovered

While an analysis of PISA is not the central focus of this book, since it is such a major contributor to the current global debate on education, it is worth reflecting upon the pros and cons of this global benchmark. PISA was launched in 2000 and its sample-based surveys of 15-year-olds take place every 3 years. In 2012, a total of 65 jurisdictions participated in PISA—which included a growing number of non-OECD countries (OECD, 2013).

One of the reasons for the increase in the popularity of PISA, it has been proposed, is the OECD's central tenet that improved educational performance leads to a better-skilled workforce and ultimately to greater economic prosperity. While there are those who challenge the foundation of this human capital argument (Brown, Lauder, & Ashton, 2010), the ability to compete in the knowledge society remains a potent and convincing rationale for policy makers and explains the continued prominence of this global test.

Even though the limitations of the PISA enterprise may not be at the forefront of the minds of those primarily tasked with raising educational performance, increasingly, there are various concerns about this international test (Johansson, 2016; Kyriakides, Georgiou, Creemers, Panayiotou, & Reynolds, 2018). Various technical and methodological issues have been highlighted, raising questions over the validity of the PISA survey results. It has also been noted that any serious consideration of cultural influences across the different education systems that are weighed and measured has been minimally explored (Alexander, 2012; Harris & Jones, 2015b).

Sahlberg (2018) has argued that the Global Education Reform Movement (GERM), with its accompanying apparatus of standardization, testing, and accountability, has largely found validation and reinforcement through PISA. Other writers have noted that powerful alliances exist between the OECD; the European Union; United Nations Educational, Scientific, and Cultural Organization (UNESCO); and the World Bank, which means a mutual reinforcement of certain ideas about educational productivity, economic efficiency, human capital, and standardization (Baird et al., 2016).

One major concern is that PISA's rankings create panic and discomfort in practically all countries, including high-scoring countries.

> This produces an urge for politicians and bureaucrats to do "something" to rectify the situation. But PISA cannot, by its "snapshot" research design, say anything about cause and effect. Hence the creativity in interpretations blossoms and educational reforms that are not at all empirically founded are introduced, often overnight. (Sjöberg, 2019, p. 14)

For those countries who fare less well in PISA, there is normally some introspection, allocation of blame, and unwelcome media attention. The media commentary follows a predictable pattern—if you don't do well on PISA, then your education system is fundamentally broken, failing, and/or in dire need of repair. Despite a rationality that says this can't be the case in all systems below the PISA Top 10, serious PISA shock quickly takes over (Baroutsis & Lingard, 2018).

PISA Shock

Following the 2012 PISA results, *The Australian* ran the following headline: "We Risk Losing Education Race, PM Warns." In this media story, the then–prime minister, Julia Gillard, was quoted as saying,

Four of the top five performing school systems in the world are in our region and they are getting better and better. . . . On average, kids at 15 in those nations are six months ahead of Australian kids at 15 and they are a year in front of the OECD mean. . . . If we are talking about today's children—tomorrow's workers—I want them to be workers in a high-skill, high-wage economy where we are still leading the world. I don't want them to be workers in an economy where we are kind of the runt of the litter in our region. (Franklin, 2012)

The number of participating countries has grown substantially since 2000, with 65 nations participating in 2012 and a 40% increase in participation rates in 2015 to 71 participating countries. These increases in the number of participating countries are rarely acknowledged in the press when discussing Australia's position in global rankings. Yet this is a fundamental piece of information. Simple mathematics would suggest that ranks are more likely to change and decrease when the number of participants changes, irrespective of any change in performance. This is ignored and neglected in media coverage, along with many other important considerations and limitations.

Most countries have some sort of "PISA game plan" to improve performance next time and a contingency position when the expected better scores fail to materialize once again. For those countries at the top of the PISA tables, the central aim is to stay there at all costs. For those countries below the PISA plumb line, there is often a cycle of blame, retribution, and regressive policies aimed at fixing the teachers and fixing the system (Evers & Kneyber, 2015).

Media coverage also tends to overgeneralize and to exalt certain education systems. For example, the Australian press did not stop referencing Finland, and its coverage also included Asian nations, especially Shanghai in 2009. the *Sydney Morning Herald* reported that "Australian policy makers could learn much from China" (Baroutsis & Lingard, 2017). The Grattan Institute Report (Jensen, 2012) also sought to draw on the high-performing East Asian nations to make policy suggestions for Australia. Despite major cultural, demographic, social, and political differences among Australia, Finland, and Shanghai (mistakenly viewed as representative of all of China), this did not prevent media commentary on Shanghai as a suitable reference system for the whole of Australian schooling.

In PISA 2012, in terms of the jurisdictions of Australia, Western Australia and the Australian Capital Territory did very well, while the Northern Territory and Tasmania performed comparatively poorly. This went largely unreported. Rather, there was a media fixation with Australia's average score and comparison with other countries in the PISA league tables.

Clear differences in performance *within* countries are shown in the PISA data, but they are rarely in receipt of any serious commentary. Other jurisdictions in China take part in PISA, but interestingly, only Shanghai, Beijing, and Hong Kong are reported. PISA data can be disaggregated by ethnicity within countries, but this information is simply not placed in the public domain, as it would show marked differences between certain groups.

While the innumerable accounts of education systems that perform well in PISA may be interesting, there has been an "unfortunate overspill into policy direction and formation" (Burdett & O'Donnell, 2016, p. 113). Concerns have been raised over the way in which PISA is being used to justify certain reform strategies and certain policies over others.

Learning from other education systems can, of course, be very useful and helpful, particularly where contextual factors and variables are fully and properly considered. Horizon scanning is important so that the same policy mistakes are not repeated by education systems and that fruitful learning across international boundaries can occur.

While looking across different countries might be interesting and even illuminating, policy makers need to pay far more attention to *within-system* differences and the inequities therein that are reflective of broader *within-country* structural inequalities. The core problem is that PISA is a major distraction. It takes policy attention away from more pressing and important educational issues within systems.

In years to come, educators will look back and wonder about the global preoccupation with PISA. They will reflect on the policy consequences of PISA and the practical consequences for those who teach and learn in schools.

BURNOUT AND OPT OUT?

All countries around the world are understandably keen to improve their education systems. As a result, there is a great deal of frenetic reform activity and collective global angst focused on securing ever-higher school and system performance. Yet the human cost of this reform juggernaut is rarely counted or fully appreciated.

Reform is an extremely disruptive and costly process in both a material and psychological sense, but there is a rhetoric that accompanies any reform process, a discourse of rationality that presents the reform in a logical, convincing, and wholly positive way. As the PISA example has already highlighted, there is a predictable sequence. Normally, there is some "evidence" that the reform is needed and that it is aimed at tackling some real or manufactured deficit in the education system. Consequently, those working in schools and classrooms receive additional work in the shape of unwanted reforms or changes.

> It's not just the mandates from the central office. It's the unintended, perverse effects of a rigid accountability system. For example, schools and staff are judged overwhelmingly on reading and math test scores. Reading and math are fundamental, but when school quality is solely based on these subjects, the result is that schools often move to de-emphasize social studies, science, and arts. We have heard this complaint most of all in elementary schools, where there is often no dedicated time and staff for these subjects. This is counterproductive. (Batchelor & Wattenberg, 2017)

Frequently, educators are attempting to implement policy changes or new reforms with limited resources, time, and support. Schools often lack the internal capacity to deliver the range of imposed changes and mandated reforms that continuously shower down on them. The constant educational policy churn can cause confusion, overload, and change fatigue as those at the chalk-face struggle to put in place the policy demands imposed upon them.

> For decades, education policy makers have been chipping away at school reform. Accountability and privatization have been the policy panaceas. It's been a demanding tour of duty, heavy on obligation and light on inspiration. In the United States and elsewhere, the threat of pressure and the promise of support too often turned out to create excessive impositions unaccompanied by meaningful assistance. The result has been an exodus of educators toward fields that offer more creativity and innovation. (Shirley, 2016, p. 1)

In a growing number of countries, teacher shortages (Richardson, 2019) tell their own story of disillusionment and, in some cases, despair. Constant policy switching and the arrival of new initiatives are not the only culprit for teacher shortages in town. Increased workload and increased scrutiny plus teacher evaluations are cited by many as the core reasons for leaving the profession. The teacher shortage is reaching a crisis point in the United States, with states grappling for the best educators (Carragher, 2018). In England, the teacher shortage problem is largely one of retaining teachers in schools despite some hefty cash incentives (Dobush, 2019). Teachers are simply burnt out, so they opt out.

While transformation and change are a necessary part of improving any education system, the sheer pace of change and the additional workload that accompanies it can prove to be overwhelming for teachers and leaders in schools. Well-being can suffer as a result of too much pressure on top of the daily task of educating children, many of whom are vulnerable or living in challenging circumstances. The pace of educational change can be too great, too quick, and—some would argue—largely focused on the wrong things.

In his work, Michael Fullan (2011) talks about the *wrong drivers* for educational change and improvement. He points toward the damage done by excessive accountability, standardization, and testing to education systems striving to be the best. He argues that competition as the main driver has proved to be most damaging and that systems weighed down by an apparatus of accountability are least likely to perform well.

Pasi Sahlberg (2018) similarly suggests that market forces do not improve schools, yet market mechanisms remain in full flight in the United States and in England. The adherence to market forces is based on the logical but fundamentally flawed belief that private involvement in schooling will secure better outcomes. Charter schools in the United States, similar to academies in England, are not demonstrating the expected benefits or outcomes. In England, the academies movement has increasingly come under fire. Charter schools and academies view excellence as the priority, with equity as an afterthought.

EQUITY: AN AFTERTHOUGHT?

The OECD countries that participate in PISA tend to be developed and wealthy; the non-OECD countries are distinctively different in this respect. This small but critically important fact explains a great deal about the winners and losers in PISA, as seen in Figure 2.1.

If you are in a school in Turkey (50) or Indonesia (62), like so many countries in the red category, how you perform at school is predominantly a function of your socioeconomic circumstance rather than the school curriculum, assessment processes, or the quality of teachers' professional learning.

Think about this for a moment: The gross national income per capita in Finland is $46,246, and 0% of its 5.5 million population earns less than $1.90 a day. The gap between the rich and poor in society is relatively small. In Indonesia, the population of 264 million people have a gross national income per capita of $3,725, and 5% of the population earns less than $1.90 a day (13.2 million); 73% of the poorest youth are out of school. In Finland, 93% of the poorest youth graduate from secondary school (United Nations Educational, Scientific, and Cultural Organization [UNESCO], n.d.).

Figure 2.1 PISA Worldwide Ranking

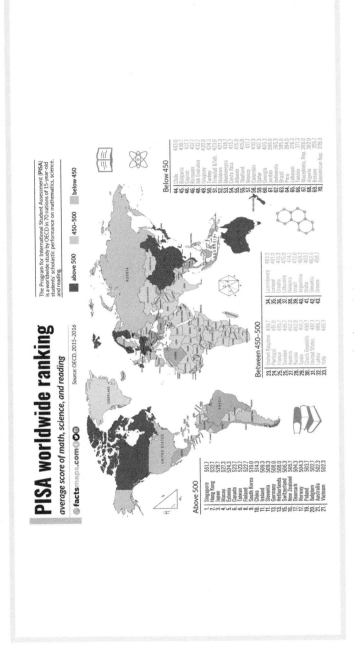

Source: PISA Worldwide Ranking Map, factsmaps.com. Printed with permission.

In Australia, the gross national income per capita is $52,355 among a population of 24.6 million people, and 0.5% of its population earns less than $1.90 a day. In Singapore, the gross national income per capita is $55,651, and 0% of its 5.5 million population earns less than $1.90 a day. In Thailand, the gross national income per capita is $6,306, and 0% of its 69 million population earns less than $1.90 a day. Such contextual differences are critically important to consider, as they explain educational differences in performance far more accurately than PISA.

In developing countries, getting teachers into schools regularly is often a significant challenge, and many primary teachers (for example, in Indonesia) are not educated to degree level. In Russia, teachers often have another job to make ends meet. This is in stark contrast to the experience of teachers in more affluent countries such as Australia, the United States, and Canada, where payment, professional development, and job security are expected.

The PISA framework and its tests are geared toward the relatively rich and modernized OECD countries. When this instrument is used as a benchmark for comparing educational standards in poorer, developing countries with large swathes of young people out of school, it is questionable whether it is possible to draw any meaningful comparisons at all.

It is also important to note that the target population of the PISA testing are the 15-year-olds who attend school. In many countries, the whole age cohort is simply not represented. For example, in China, the children of migrant workers do not participate in PISA, which means that in cities such as Shanghai or Beijing, the sampling is ultimately representative of the more affluent city dwellers and is therefore not a representative sample.

Similarly, when Vietnam is heralded as a "stunning school success" based on PISA scores, the fact that only 56% of their 15-year-old cohort attends schools and is eligible for the PISA sample is conveniently ignored. About a third of Shanghai's 15-year-olds are excluded from the test, a fact that was for a long time denied by the PISA organizers.

In terms of inequity, a neglected issue is the students who are exempt. Singapore, South Korea, and China do not include special needs children into mainstream education, as many other countries do. For most OECD countries, nearly all 15-year-olds attend school and hence are part of the target population to be sampled for testing. This raises all sorts of questions about the children who are left out of PISA and are left behind.

A report by the orchestrator of PISA, Andreas Schleicher, maps the development and the successes of PISA in *World Class: Building a 21st Century School System* (OECD, 2018) and rehearses many of the well-known arguments for this international assessment and, by association, its preferred reform strategies. In the book, he argues that "one of the most important insights from PISA was that education systems could be changed and *made* to perform." It is also proposed that culture is not necessarily an important consideration when addressing reform at scale. He cites the success of many countries, such as Mexico, Germany, Colombia, and Peru, that have improved their performance irrespective of their context and their culture.

There are two important observations to be made here. Firstly, the term *world-class* is relatively meaningless because it is not possible to say that a practice is *good, best,* or *effective* in all settings, on all occasions, and with all students.

Secondly, by citing countries such as Mexico, Colombia, and Peru, there is the implication that other countries that are also facing an uphill struggle to improve educational outcomes can easily follow their well-trodden pathway to success. Far less is said in the book about countries that have failed to make any real progress in PISA, despite borrowing some of the strategies of the more-successful performers. The countries who have failed to lift their performance tend not to make the OECD headlines and are not singled out for consideration.

Fast-forward to the present day and the OECD has realized the need to turn up the equity part of its global agenda. It is now promoting reports based on data that offer insights into how countries perform in terms of student well-being and equity. Equity in education (OECD, 2018) highlights that

- higher income inequality and lower levels of social mobility tend to go together;
- education can promote social mobility, but this varies across countries;
- wealthier countries have benefited from the expansion of access to education;
- expansion in education does not result in greater equity; and
- upward educational mobility varies from country to country.

Much of the report talks about the impact of disadvantage on educational attainment, but it is proposed that poverty need not be destiny. For example, 10% of the most deprived children in the Dominican Republic outperformed children from similar backgrounds in Latin America. Less is said, however, about whether they outperformed young people in wealthier contexts. The net explanation given for this quite remarkable relative performance gain is "resiliency."

The implication of the "resiliency" argument is that children from developing countries merely need to be more resilient to succeed as the young people in the Dominican Republic have. How resilient can a young person be who is living in acute poverty with insufficient food, clothing, and care? Suggesting that resiliency is the answer locates fault and responsibility with the child and not the system.

Later in this book, the structural barriers to equity and the way they manifest themselves in various systems will be outlined in far more depth, but for now, let's stay with the idea of system change and how it affects equity.

SYSTEM CHANGE AND EQUITY

The statement that "there is no improvement without change but not all change leads to improvement" (Fullan, 2009) could not be more apposite or true in the pursuit of better system performance today. When thinking about system change, however, it is important to note that there is not one coherent system but that multiple, inherently complex and convoluted systems exist. No one strategy or approach will or can work everywhere.

Pursuing what works may be important, but in terms of system-level change, the strategies that are considered to work in one context are unlikely to work perfectly, or indeed at all, in another setting (Harris & Jones, 2015a). Inevitably, there are a multifaceted set of factors plus substantial differences across educational systems, political systems, societies, and cultures that interact, both positively and negatively, on any reform process.

Also, as noted earlier, the side effects of certain policy decisions and approaches are often factored out or ignored (Zhao, 2017, 2018). One of the side effects, it could be argued, is inequity. The exclusion of certain groups of children is devastatingly inequitable but seems not to make the media headlines. What is promoted, however, are accounts of the best performers.

For example, a World Bank report (Liang, Kidwai, & Zhang, 2016) that focused on Shanghai's PISA success noted that teachers are supported with professional development, which is collaborative in nature and is focused upon improving instruction through a clear framework of learning standards, regular student assessment, and a well-aligned curriculum. The report adds that "one of the most impressive aspects of the Shanghai system is the way it grooms, supports and manages teachers who are central to any effort to raise the education quality in schools" (Liang et al., 2016).

This report then lists a range of factors that actively help teachers in Shanghai to improve—and which, by implication, could be useful to other education systems. In addition, the report notes that "it will increasingly be important for Shanghai to find a healthier balance between academic excellence and students' social and emotional well-being" (Liang et al., 2016).

This is the only hint, in the entire report, that there are certain human trade-offs and negative implications of being the best placed in PISA. What exactly do we know about improving system performance and the consequences for equity?

In order to understand how and why certain education systems outperform others, a much closer look at their approaches to equity and inclusion is necessary. Greater attention needs to be paid to some of the hidden aspects that make educational success or failure more or less likely. The central proposition is that equity will remain in the shadow of excellence if policy attention remains fixated with narrow measures of performance.

The pages that follow exemplify why equity and equality cannot simply be sidelined from any serious consideration or analysis of school and system performance. The effects of poverty on academic, social, and emotional health are clearly documented and well established (Whitty & Anders, 2017). The next chapter looks at the root causes of inequity and explores some hard truths. It explains why inequity prevails and persists.

CHAPTER
3

Hard Truths

By 2030, ensure that all girls and boys complete free, equitable and quality primary and secondary education leading to relevant and effective learning outcomes.

Sustainable Development Goals (2015)

Inequality and inequity are not only hardwired into many education systems but are also widely accepted, exploited, and in some cases, actively maintained (Harris & Jones, 2017). For many education systems, closing the poverty and attainment gap is a stated policy priority. In other education systems, breaking the powerful link between poverty and underachievement remains a daunting and challenging prospect. The effects of poverty on young people are multifaceted, affecting self-esteem, mental health, and participation in wider society.

Income inequities also play out in different ways that directly affect educational attainment and opportunities. For example, more-affluent young people can quite simply purchase additional tutoring and obtain a comparative advantage (Bray & Lykins, 2012). In Singapore (Yang, 2016), South Korea (Financial Times, n.d.), and Hong Kong (Martin, 2015), the private tutoring system is highly profitable, as young people in many parts of Asia strive to achieve in ways that are culturally expected.

More-affluent parents, it seems, can also buy places in the most sought-after universities. In the United States, a major scandal broke when it emerged that a California company had made over $25 million from parents seeking places for their children in top schools, including Georgetown University, Stanford University, and Yale University (Barrett & Zapotosky, 2019). Fifty people, including 33 parents and athletics coaches, were criminally charged in the nation's largest known college admissions scandal. One prominent Hollywood star and her husband were accused of paying $500,000 in a scheme that involved cheating on college entrance exams and bribing athletic coaches to secure a place at the University of Southern California.

The attorney general presiding over the case said,

> These parents are a catalog of wealth and privilege. This case is about the widening corruption of elite college admissions through the steady application of wealth combined with fraud. There can be no separate college admission system for the wealthy, and I'll add there will not be a separate criminal justice system, either.

Buying places at a university does not only concern the wealthiest parents/families in the United States but is also part of a global phenomenon in which access to education is readily available to purchase. For rich kids, the business of purchasing essays (Yorke, 2017) and dissertations is booming, offering them the chance of higher grades and better degree outcomes. For the children of the poor, their experiences of education could not be further apart.

INEQUITY AND POVERTY

One profound correlate of growing up in a very poor household is nonattendance at school. For millions of children living in poverty, attending school is simply not an option. The available data on "out of school" children show that in Indonesia, on average, 1,335,753 primary-aged children are out of school. In the Philippines, the available data show that approximately 1,223,909 primary-aged children are not enrolled in any school.

Living in poverty means that children work to provide extra income for their families and more frequently look after younger siblings rather than attending school. In this way, poverty determines participation in schooling and, in turn, subsequently affects educational achievement and attainment. In developing countries, poverty and income inequality constitute a significant determinant of participation in schooling. In short, poverty deeply affects uneven participation and engagement in education.

Economic and social inequities remain potent and pervasive influences on schooling. For school leaders in areas of high deprivation, their daily challenge is to alleviate some of the more negative influences that accompany poverty through the school gates. Family problems follow children into the classroom, and for teachers, these problems are often detrimental to learning and teaching. For school leaders, the daily decisions about the well-being, safety, and care of children can be relentless and often distressing. School leaders are on the front line, often making incredibly hard choices that directly affect vulnerable and at-risk children and their families.

Despite many challenges and difficulties, schools in some of the most disadvantaged circumstances continue to succeed against the odds. Chapter 4 considers such schools and explores how certain inequities can be overcome by those leading in schools and classrooms. There is a wealth of research evidence that shows how young people facing hardship and family difficulties achieve in school and subsequently move onto promising careers. The stubborn bond between disadvantage and underachievement can be broken, but this is only secured through the determination and dedication of educators working together with the community.

For so many young people living in poverty, school may be their only hope of feeling valued and nurtured. Increasingly, children come into schools in need of mental health support and specialist care (Mental Health Foundation, n.d.). The job of school leaders and teachers, therefore, has never been tougher or more important.

Schools, however, cannot tackle the net results of poverty alone. Interagency work is critical if some of the more complex issues that so many children face are to be dealt with properly. Collaboration among different professional groups is essential if the diverse challenges facing families are to be addressed. Teachers and school leaders can only do so much.

CONTEXT MATTERS

Opportunity for all remains an acute challenge for school and system leaders in high-poverty contexts. A report published in the early morning of the 21st of December 2017 by the Education Policy Institute (Andrews & Perera, 2017) highlighted that in England, there is an acute north and south educational divide. The report signaled that access to high-performing schools has become more unequal and geographically divided.

It stated that areas with "consistently low densities of high-performing schools" were all outside London and the south east. Essentially, if you are a pupil in Blackpool, Hartlepool, Barnsley, Redcar, Cleveland, Knowsley, and Middlesbrough, your chances of attending a high-performing school are significantly lower than anywhere else in the country. The report states that of particular note is the north east, which, as a region, has virtually no high-performing schools.

These areas face significant barriers in accessing a high-performing or effective school. Moreover, local authorities that have experienced the greatest increases in the density of high-performing school places between 2010 and 2015 are overwhelmingly concentrated in London, which already had a relatively high density of high-performing school places.

Even with such alarming findings, this report has not received the media attention it clearly deserves and warrants. It seems to have faded away, along with its stark implication of deep-rooted structural inequity. Geographical inequity has profound consequences for young people and their life chances.

Charter schools are now a growing part of K–12 education in the United States. Charter schools are public schools that are granted operational autonomy by their authorizing agency in return for a commitment to achieve performance levels specified in a contract. Similar to traditional public schools, charter schools are prohibited from charging tuition, must not discriminate in admissions or be religious in their operation or affiliation, and are overseen by a public entity.

Unlike traditional public schools, however, most charters are open to all students who wish to apply, regardless of where they live. Most charter schools are independent of the traditional public school district in which they operate. Evidence from a study by DeAngelis, Wolf, Maloney, and May (2018) found that public charter schools received an average of $5,721, or about 29%, less per pupil than traditional public schools. This study represents the latest evidence regarding remaining public charter school funding inequities where charters are most common: in cities.

The authors conclude that it is only with equal total funding of students in public education can we be confident that children will not be *valued less* simply because of their circumstances. There is now a body of emerging evidence highlighting how charter schools are contributing to inequity and the greater segregation of young people. In short, for those children most in need, charter schools are simply not delivering.

The education playing field is far from level for young people who live in deprived contexts and experience the effects of poverty on a daily basis (Harris & Jones, 2018). For those leading schools in challenging circumstances in such locations, this simply adds to the daily uphill struggle facing teachers and leaders alike.

LEADING FOR EQUITY

If there is a clear political will and commitment to actively deal with inequity, then those leading classrooms and schools have at least a fighting chance. If the converse is true and the political climate is promoting educational reforms that are punitive, devaluing, and disempowering, then the tide of structural inequality and inequity will not turn.

As Darling-Hammond made clear over a decade ago,

> if academic outcomes for minority and low-income children are to change, reforms must alter the quality and quantity of learning opportunities they encounter. To improve achievement, school reforms must assure access to high-quality teaching within the context of a rich and challenging curriculum, supported by personalized schools and classes. Accomplishing such a goal will require equalization of financial resources, changes in curriculum and testing policies, and improvements in the supply of highly qualified teachers to all students. (2007, p. 329)

This remains so true. While there are no simple solutions, it is increasingly clear that without a clear and central policy commitment to tackling inequity, the work of those who are leading schools becomes far harder. International evidence shows that equity should not be an afterthought in education reform; it should not be an add-on or a follow-on—it must be *the* policy priority (Harris & Jones, 2018). In the moving and prophetic words of a leading Canadian educator and global champion of equity, Dr. Avis Glase, "the children cannot wait" (Benns, 2017).

Leading for Equity tells the compelling story of the Montgomery County (Maryland) Public Schools (MCPS) system and its transformation in less than a decade into a system committed to breaking the links among race, class, and academic achievement. The story starts with a visionary superintendent but does not end there. The story is essentially one of distributed leadership, including community leadership and a collective commitment to deal with issues of equity head-on. MCPS serves a population of 140,000 students who come from 163 different countries and speak 134 different languages (Childress, Doyle, & Thomas, 2009).

This story is centrally one of community empowerment and engagement. Like so many accounts of school and system turnaround, it is an account of a relentless and determined drive by those leading at all levels to close the attainment gap and to give all children opportunities for success. Yet such leadership does not exist within a policy vacuum (Breakspear, Peterson, Alfadala, & Khair, 2017). The policy context in which students, teachers, and school leaders find themselves is a critical determinant of their success or failure.

One way forward, as an alternative to seeking temporary policy solutions, is to prioritize and systematically address some of the real barriers to better school and system performance. For example, high levels of poverty, deep inequalities in the system, and serious levels of disadvantage make it highly unlikely that any interventions, however well intentioned, will properly tackle inequity.

The challenge is simply too big, and the causes of inequity are too complex. As Sahlberg and Hasak (2016) suggest, it is possible that we are simply looking in the wrong place to find our explanations for system performance and that piecemeal strategies borrowed from other countries are not the answer.

Without question, it is time to take a long, hard look at the reasons why schools and school systems perform as they do. This will mean facing some hard truths about variations in educational performance and the real reasons for continued inequities.

HARD TRUTH 1—PRIVATIZATION

It has been argued that the private sector's role in education has many advantages over the traditional public delivery of education. Realizing such benefits, however, depends greatly on regulatory frameworks and the way in which governments oversee various partnerships with the private sector (World Bank, 2009). Although governments remain the main financiers of education, at least of primary and secondary education, in many countries, private companies now deliver a sizable proportion of education. Education as a private good has certainly been one reason for a preoccupation with testing and has unleashed a range of commercial opportunities for big corporations.

For the past decade, the United States has been at the forefront of market-driven reforms in education, including private–public partnerships (PPPs). In Organization for Economic Cooperation and Development (OECD) countries, more than 20% of public education expenditure goes to private institutions and about 12% is spent on privately managed institutions (Patrinos, 2011). While private sector involvement in education has its strengths, the evidence also highlights that without strong systems of accountability, private schools with public funding may find it a challenge to produce the gains expected or anticipated. In education systems across Asia, PPPs are flourishing.

Private Sector Intervention

PPPs are far from a new phenomenon. The scale of private sector intervention, however, particularly in developing countries in Asia, is rapidly increasing. One of the largest private providers of education is now the most powerful multinational education corporation in the world. For Pearson, the global "crisis" in education has presented a lucrative business opportunity. As the CEO of Pearson, John Fallon (2015) notes, "the bigger Pearson's social impact—the more we can create a faster growing and more profitable company and do so in a sustainable manner."

Pearson's venture into the Philippines is possibly the clearest indication yet that this major for-profit organization is now moving its commercial operation eastward. Within Asia, there are many countries that are developing and impoverished and where vast income inequalities exist. Countries such as the Philippines, Indonesia, and Cambodia have enormous challenges facing them in areas of education and social reform. They are also a soft target for large-scale, private sector intervention.

The brand of market-led education reform, exemplified by Pearson and some other private sector providers, is now being shipped to countries that can least afford them and where the infrastructure to make them work simply does not exist.

In February 2018, tens of thousands of teachers from West Virginia launched a strike demanding better public education in the face of years of austerity. A year later, teachers union leaders from across Africa gathered in Addis Ababa for a meeting of African Union heads of state with a demand to halt the move toward privatized education and to provide inclusive and equitable, quality, free public education for all. Even though these teachers were an ocean apart, their fight against the privatization of schooling was the same.

Bridge International Academies (Dearden, 2018) is a network of private pre-primary and primary schools operating across Africa and Asia using what it calls the "school in a box" model, a highly standardized approach with scripted lessons that teachers must deliver mechanically, word by word. Bridge draws investment from educational multinationals such as Pearson, Bill Gates, the World Bank, and the British Department for International Development (DfID).

Although these schools are said to be low cost, they are far too expensive for many parents/families. In Kenya, Uganda, and Nigeria, the fees to attend the schools were significantly higher than the $6 per month claimed by the company. In Kenya, tuition fees alone ranged from $6.40 to $10.57 a month. The monthly costs, when uniforms are added in, jump to an average of over $17 per month, well out of reach of poorer families.

On the website of the Bridge International Academies (Bridge, n.d.), it states that "Bridge believes every child has the right to high quality education." In stark contrast, there is evidence (Edwards, 2018) of low-quality educational provision and mass exploitation of the poorest parents/families and communities.

HARD TRUTH 2—CONTEXT AND CULTURE MATTER

In 2014, the United Kingdom government announced that 32 hub schools would ensure that English students reached the same level as their Eastern peers. The hub schools hosted Chinese teachers who ran master classes; two years later, the school standards minister announced that the South Asian "mastery" approach to teaching math was set to become a standard part of the primary curriculum.

£41 million was aimed at ensuring that 8,000 primary schools utilized the approach used by some of the leading performers in math in the world, including Shanghai, Singapore, and Hong Kong.

Criticism of this approach was leveled at the lack of consideration of cultural and contextual aspects. Professor Yong Zhao argued that it was not possible to recreate school systems and teaching techniques outside the culture and context in which they were developed (Roberts, 2018).

> Even if you could recreate all of the characteristics that you find in Shanghai today or in Singapore it would take 15 years to transfer this. And at the end, you would be left recreating what people were doing in Shanghai 15 years ago. Why would you want to turn to another country's past to decide your future? That seems to me to be a stupid idea.

The idea of using math textbooks from China in English classrooms has attracted much media attention worldwide (Qin, 2017). Little is said, however, about the more negative aspects of the Chinese education system or the pressure exacted on Chinese children to learn (Liu, 2016).

> In China, schoolchildren are anything but casual Sunday learners. They drill daily and they're required to reach full literacy (in Chinese) astonishingly quickly. . . . The process itself drills rigidity and memorization into a child's routine; some education watchers say it's the unforgiving task of learning Chinese itself that lays the groundwork to killing curiosity and creativity in the Chinese schoolchild. (Chu, 2017, p. 86)

The hard truth is that culture and context explain a great deal about differential educational performance.

Language

One very important cultural difference is language. In many countries, there is great pride and substantial investment in promoting and sustaining indigenous languages. Hence, many young people are taught in a language other than English. In Singapore, the main language of instruction is English, and most young people in Singapore have high levels of English proficiency very early on in their school career. This may seem like a small contextual difference, but it is one that is critically important in explaining differential performance and different career trajectories for young people in different countries.

A proficiency in English opens doors in many countries. Additionally, in the future, good communication skills and language proficiency increasingly will define access to employment in the global marketplace. English is the language of globalization in its various guises. As well as being the common language of global commerce and international tourism, English is the language of more specialized forms of globalization, including aviation, information technology, and diplomacy, for example.

Beyond being the world's preferred common language, English is also an Asian language in both a demographic and an official sense. Asia has approximately 800 million English speakers, and English is particularly widespread in China and India. Young people who are not proficient in English will consequently find themselves at some disadvantage.

Indonesia is a vast, sprawling education system dispersed over a large archipelago. The challenge of English language acquisition therefore is inherently more daunting than in tiny education systems such as Singapore or Hong Kong. In addition, as with many of the larger education systems in Asia, there is great cultural, religious, and ethnic diversity that works in its own way to reformulate, redesign, and sometimes undermine approaches to education reform, especially those borrowed and imposed from elsewhere.

Context and culture remain potent variables in any improvement mix, whether at the classroom, school, or system level. Cultural influences are not some inconvenient background noise, as some would contend, but rather are powerful influences that can make or break any well-intentioned policy or intervention. This is not to imply that in the face of contextual and cultural forces, there is little that can be done to improve schools or systems, but simply to note that within the interdependent and inter-reliant dynamics of transformation and change, culture and context play a significant role.

HARD TRUTH 3—INEQUALITY

Turning to the next hard truth, it is widely accepted and proven that inequality makes a profound and significant difference to education outcomes and performance. The stark reality is that the stubborn bond between disadvantage and underachievement is difficult to break. It should come as no surprise, therefore, that education performance in the Philippines or Cambodia or Indonesia is significantly lower than that of Singapore or Hong Kong or South Korea. A quick look at the economic performance and wealth distribution of different countries within the Asian region will tell you everything you need to know.

Levels of poverty and degrees of inequality within a country have an acute impact on educational outcomes. Therefore, the OECD's (2018) idea of simply being "resilient" is both misguided and inherently problematic. One profound consequence of disadvantage is that for many young people in the most impoverished settings, attending school is simply not an option. Unlike the richer countries, where attendance is an important indicator of a school's performance, in developing countries, nonattendance can be a norm, as it is more often the case that children work to provide extra income for their families or help look after younger siblings than attend school.

Despite yawning gaps in wealth and significant income differentials between countries, the same expectations of competing globally are imposed upon schools and school systems. Scratch the surface of educational underperformance and you will find poverty and inequality firmly hand in hand.

In terms of inequality, the differences in *perceived* inequalities between people in different countries has been captured by Hofstede's Power Distance Index (PDI). This reflects the degree to which a culture is comfortable with power inequities, as seen in Figure 3.1.

Figure 3.1 Power Distance World Map

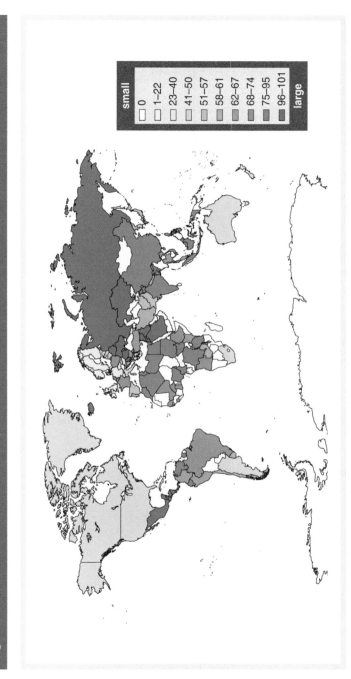

small
0
1–22
23–40
41–50
51–57
58–61
62–67
68–74
75–95
96–101
large

Source: Power Distance World Map, Hofstede, G., Hofstede, G. J., Minkove, M., *Cultures and Organizations: Software of the Mind*, McGraw Hill (2010). Printed with permission.

The higher the PDI number, the greater the power distance, meaning that members of a culture expect and accept that power is distributed unequally. At the top of the PDI is Malaysia, with an index of 104. This means that people in Malaysia accept a hierarchical order with everyone in their place, which does not require justification, even though there are deep and obvious inequalities. The Philippines' scores are also high (94), as are the scores of China (80), Indonesia (78), and India (77). The United States (40), Canada (39), Great Britain (35), and Sweden (31) score significantly lower. The PDI data show that inequality in society is not only a feature of many countries but is also widely accepted and tolerated.

Private Tutoring

Such inequalities play out in different ways in different contexts. However, one glaring inequality, particularly in Asian countries, is the ability to capitalize upon the comparative advantage of private tutoring. In Singapore, parents/families spend 1 billion Singapore dollars a year on private tutoring. In South Korea, young people go to school twice a day, visiting private tutors after formal schooling ends to prep and practice until the early hours of the morning.

In Hong Kong, the private tutoring system is also big business, as young people strive to achieve in ways that are both culturally expected and self-imposed. In stark contrast, for those less-affluent countries, the possibility of private tutoring is a distant dream. The available financial resource is used for survival—day in, day out—and almost never used to invest in education.

The third hard truth is that inequality remains a powerful determinant of educational success or failure. Those with material means not only have access to a high-quality education but can also buy additional support when and in what form they need it. In short, the wealthy have a greater chance of success; by contrast, the children of the poor, marginalized, or excluded simply do not have the means or the access to such privileges.

This is not new news. Without question, many reform efforts have been very effective in turning the tide on poverty, inequality, and underachievement. The aim is not to negate or belittle their substantive and successful efforts. Instead, it is simply to say that economic and social inequities remain potent and pervasive influences on education achievement and attainment, despite resilient teachers and students.

HARD TRUTH 4—POLITICS AND CORRUPTION

This is possibly the most dangerous hard truth of all, particularly in certain countries and under certain regimes. It is to acknowledge and identify that education is part of a political machine and as such is not free from centralized control or corruption. In many countries, education remains a highly politicized and political process. Many schools operate in strictly controlled systems where there is little latitude for any innovation or change that is not authorized or approved by the government.

Within such systems, teaching and education remain a powerful form of social reproduction and a prime way of establishing the dominant cultural identity, religion, norms, and values. For example, in Malaysia, the state-set curriculum requires many courses to incorporate political material, meaning there is simply not enough time and resources to teach mathematics, reading, and science well. Students in some schools are required to learn three languages, receive religious instruction, and study many courses on Malaysian history and society. These are designed to promote acceptance of the Barisan Nasional narrative about the optimal type of social–economic–political arrangements for Malaysia, such as Ketuanan Melayu (Malay supremacy).

These politically motivated courses promote recitation by students of state-set viewpoints rather than critical examination by students. This politicization of the school curriculum means that the overall tone in Malaysian schools is conformity to orthodoxy rather than creative thinking that produces knowledge-led growth (Woo, 2019).

In the most authoritarian education systems, challenging traditional views and established norms is culturally unacceptable and viewed as questioning or challenging those in authority. This may bring its own brand of consequences and a punitive set of outcomes. In some countries, nepotism and corruption define and dictate how business is enacted. This inevitably spills over into education. Large-scale lucrative contracts are issued, only to be captured by the same organization—the usual group of suspects.

Corruption

As one overseas consultant explained,

> The text book publishing business is the area in the school system where there is the greatest financial corruption. It provides one of the biggest recurring markets in many African countries, a market that is never satiated, as year after year new textbooks are needed for the new group of students. There is intense competition from international publishers, much of it involving diverse forms of corruption. Text books in much of francophone Africa cost up to ten times that of similar texts published in Asia. As only officially sanctioned texts can be used in schools, the potential for corruption is great. (Bennett, 2001)

If only this were a rare episode, an outlier, an infrequent occurrence—but unfortunately, it is not. A global corruption report (Transparency International, 2013) highlights that the illicit nature of corruption makes it difficult to measure its cost to education in purely financial terms. It is also often difficult to distinguish between corruption and inefficiency and mismanagement in schools and universities. Furthermore, the report proposes that those who possess power and resources will strive to capture the benefits of education for themselves and their families. Elites often reproduce existing power relations through schooling. Corruption becomes endemic when people engage in corrupt behaviors because they are widespread, and they feel that they cannot afford to be honest.

Issues of political integrity and corruption tend not to be as center stage in the global debate on education reform. It is easier—far easier—to imagine that all education systems are the same, devoid of the more unpalatable forms of subtle and not-so-subtle oppression and victimization. For those engaged in upbeat and hyped conversations about innovation and world-class standards or 21st-century skills, the dark side of education reform is invisible or simply ignored.

In certain countries, the political grip on education is so strong that any changes or challenges to the existing status quo may be construed as divisive or disruptive and dealt with accordingly.

WHERE NEXT?

It is not suggested in any way that these hard truths are not known. They are. Numerous writers, commentators, and critics have raised these issues in various ways. Instead, the fact is that such truths still tend to be downgraded or marginalized in the contemporary discourse about comparing educational performance. The implications are threefold:

- Firstly, the wrong reform levers are repeatedly pulled;
- Secondly, strategies for educational improvement address the consequences, not the root causes of low performance; and
- Thirdly, the negation of important contextual factors is a fundamental blind spot in any reform process aimed at equity and excellence in education.

So what follows is not a manifesto, a plan, or anything like a well-formulated framework for action. Instead, it is a series of five points that suggest a different way of thinking about and grappling with the challenge of ensuring that education reform makes a positive difference to inequity and inequality.

1. **Borrow design principles, not policies.** The limitations of policy borrowing are fairly well known and established. The evidence base on successful policy borrowing is far from conclusive and points toward the need for more contextualized and culturally embedded approaches. One way forward, therefore, would be to

extract the design principles of a successful or effective policy and import those principles into an education system in need of improvement. In this way, key principles can be adopted, adapted, and custom-made to fit specific contextual and cultural needs.

2. Focus on countries that are similar, not different. The past few years have seen increasing interest and scrutiny of the "high-performing" education systems that bring their own brand of educational utopia. While benchmarking with the high flyers may be useful and insightful, many of the high-performing countries such as Singapore or South Korea look remarkably unlike other countries. What if countries were benchmarked against those in context or culture (or at least somewhat close)? In that way, some of the stark cultural differences could be put aside, and instead, strategies used in countries that were culturally and contextually closer could be more meaningful and impactful.

3. Learn from education systems on the move. There is a tendency to look and learn from those education systems that have proven their ability to perform in international comparative assessments. As noted earlier, in many ways, this is a popular but flawed strategy. So, why not look more closely at systems on the move, those beginning to show more than the green shoots of transformation and change? These could be identified by looking at the international policy literature and within-country accounts. While the narratives of high performers may be insightful, the stories of systems on the move, those moving onward and upward, may be practically far more helpful and useful. To emulate the best is difficult; to follow in the tailwind of those accelerating a little faster is easier.

4. Focus on within-country solutions, not ready-made solutions. No education system is perfect; there are always areas for improvement. Similarly, within every education system, there are pockets of excellence—things that are done well, things that could be extended or expanded. Sharing and spreading good practices within countries would seem to be an obvious approach to improvement rather than seeking ready-made solutions from elsewhere. Building capacity within a system rather than borrowing ideas or capacity from elsewhere would seem not only cost-effective but potentially impactful.

5. Treat inequity as the root cause of educational failure. While other contributions to educational failure exist, inequity remains the most pervasive and pernicious offender. Yet policy makers tend to look for strategies or neat solutions to fix part of the problem rather than addressing the twin issues of inequity and inequality. This doesn't imply that we stop the smaller micro attempts at addressing the problem but rather that we cannot rely on those micro solutions to redress the balance.

Those charged with education reform need to take a long, hard look at the structural inequities at the macro level that make the micro solutions much less likely to work. If we accept that inequity is *the* root cause of educational failure then we should find ways to reduce that inequity, then resources, policies, and income redistribution should follow.

Some of the micro-level solutions that actively help to address educational inequity are explored next. The chapters that follow consider some of the processes and practices at the school level that can help eradicate barriers to learning.

CHAPTER

4

Leading for Equity

The process never ends. There is no single mountain to climb. At the top of one peak is another just beyond.

Richard DeLorenzo (2010)

The 20th-century writer Eli Khamarov famously said, "Poverty is like a punishment for a crime you did not commit." This is unquestionably the reality for many young people in so many countries. Equitable education is one way of redressing this punishment. Equity in education implies that any differences in learner outcomes do not result from socioeconomic differences but reflect differences in ability, skill, or aptitude to learning. A school system that is *equitable* is essentially one where all students reach their full potential, irrespective of their starting point or background.

Leading for equity is fundamentally concerned with fairness and inclusion, ensuring that all young people meet their full potential.

It means that no child is placed outside schooling (for whatever reason) and has the same access to learning opportunities.

Unfortunately, many young people go to schools that are less than effective and are ill-equipped to meet individual student needs. Such schools often face huge resource challenges, high turnover of staff, and persistent cycles of teacher shortages. For young people from poor backgrounds, their choice of school remains limited. Unlike their wealthier peers, they cannot move to a new school in a more-affluent area or choose to attend a private school. That simply isn't an option. Normally, they attend their local school that, in most cases, serves a high proportion of students who come from similar backgrounds.

If that school is less effective or struggling, for any reason, these young people become doubly disadvantaged and their progress to an appropriate level of achievement will become harder. It becomes even more imperative, therefore, that young people living in areas of deprivation attend a good or effective school. Evidence shows that schools have more of an effect on young people from deprived backgrounds, simply because they provide some of the social capital that wealthier children naturally accumulate (Chapman, Muijs, Reynolds, Sammons, & Teddlie, 2016).

This chapter looks specifically at how schools located in difficult or challenging circumstances provide effective education for all. It takes a micro look at how inequity and inequality can be addressed through changes *within* schools, recognizing, however, that schools alone cannot solve all the problems that inequity brings.

In many education systems, closing the poverty and attainment gap remains a stated policy priority and a clear aspiration. In other education systems, breaking the powerful grip of poverty on underachievement remains an unlikely prospect not only because of the sheer scale of the task but also because of adverse cultural and contextual influences.

Even though policy makers may go to great lengths to ensure they endorse equality, social justice, and fairness, there remain huge variations in wealth distribution and differential levels of equality.

As Chapter 3 outlined, economic and social inequities remain potent and pervasive influences on education achievement and attainment. For leaders of schools in areas of high poverty, the daily challenge to alleviate some of the more negative influences of poverty that young people bring through the school gates is considerable.

IMPROVING SCHOOLS IN CHALLENGING CIRCUMSTANCES

The connection between poverty and low attainment plays out dramatically in schools located in deprived areas. Improving the fortunes of schools in high-poverty settings is an uphill challenge for school leaders in many education systems (Meyers & Darwin, 2017). Schools serving areas of socioeconomic disadvantage can have a myriad of problems. These include poor facilities, fragile leadership, insufficient teaching resources, and variable teaching quality (Chapman & Harris, 2004).

Many schools in areas of high poverty are locked into the perpetuation of low community expectations of what can be achieved through the formal process of schooling. This is a common feature of many schools in areas of acute deprivation. There are also external compounding factors that make the extent of the challenge facing these schools more severe.

For example, the geographical isolation of rural schools in high-poverty settings compounds the problem of raising attainment (Davies & Halsey, 2019). In addition, punitive accountability processes, inadequate support, and poor employment opportunities make the prospect of long-term sustained improvement in such school settings less achievable. This is not to suggest that schools in such circumstances cannot improve but simply to acknowledge that the task facing them is significantly harder and potentially more daunting than schools in more favorable socioeconomic circumstances.

The cocktail of disadvantage offers a powerful explanation for the persistent inequalities in educational outcomes of pupils living in areas where family income levels are low. In such schools, pupil behavior is more challenging; teachers find that they need to deal with more social difficulties and that there is less home support for learning (Clegg, Allen, Fernandes, Freedman, & Kinnock, 2017).

The emotional strain of teaching in more-disadvantaged schools can be considerable. Furthermore, the dual threat of accountability pressure in the form of external inspection judgments and test results that fall below accepted standards acutely affect those teaching in more-disadvantaged contexts.

It may be understandable, therefore, that experienced and well-qualified teachers prefer to take jobs in less-challenging environments, that high-deprivation schools have fewer applicants for jobs, and that those who do work in more-challenging schools might continue their job search while working with a view to moving to a less-challenging school in the future.

But while it is impossible for schools to succeed against such odds, they can buck the trend. Many schools facing difficult and challenging circumstances add significant value to student achievement and learning. There is evidence to show that these schools consistently improve levels of student performance and achievement, despite the challenges they face. This is an example:

Cabramatta High School lies in the southwest area of Sydney, Australia. The school draws from a low socioeconomic and high non-English-speaking background community. With 55 languages spoken, the school hosts an intensive English center for students who are newly arrived in the country.

Creating an equitable platform for students and the community is a strong focus of the school and it attracts additional government funding to address equity, which is translated into strategies to meet the educational needs of all students. The school uses evaluation and assessment data as well as research to inform and develop strategies that are contextually specific. The mainstream high school has students of all ability levels, including gifted and talented.

When students receive their results from national literacy and numeracy tests, each student is mentored by a teacher to understand their results and develop an individual plan for growth. The school makes available resources not otherwise accessible to meet these plans. A speech pathologist, an after-school study center with tutoring, literacy lessons, and master classes are some of the additional resources that can be accessed by students.

Throughout the school, there is an emphasis on high expectations and student engagement. Professional learning is targeted to ensure that student needs are met and that teachers have access to a wide range of strategies. The community is engaged and there is a united emphasis on school achievement and creating a positive future for all young people.

School performance and results indicate consistent growth in national testing results; 85% of students access tertiary education at the completion of secondary schooling, which is significantly higher than the national average. Student retention to completion of the Higher School Certificate is substantially above state rates. Attendance levels are high, demonstrating positive student engagement.

Cabramatta is a vibrant school with programs and projects that respond to all student needs. Through all stakeholders uniting to focus on common goals and high expectations, positive student outcomes academically, in citizenship, and in social development are possible.

Beth Godwin
Principal
Cabramatta High School

In order to achieve and sustain improvement, the leaders in these schools usually exceed what might be termed as *normal efforts*. Teachers in such schools tend to work harder than their peers in more favorable socioeconomic circumstances because of the emotional and behavioral difficulties that accompany young people into school.

Despite such challenges and difficulties, evidence shows that young people facing hardship and family difficulties can achieve in school and move on to promising careers. They succeed against the odds through the determination and dedication of educators who work relentlessly with the community to ensure equitable educational opportunities for all students from all backgrounds.

SUCCEEDING AGAINST THE ODDS

The job of school leaders and teachers has never been tougher or more important. There are schools everywhere that are succeeding against the odds and there is now a great deal of evidence about practical ways of narrowing the attainment gap (Chapman, 2019; Chapman et al., 2016). Improving the effectiveness of schools in socioeconomically disadvantaged areas, however, is far from an easy job. Leadership at all levels must be exceptional, with a collective determination to succeed. But what exactly does it take to succeed against the odds?

What follows is a summary of approaches that international evidence suggests work in practice. These are offered not as a prescriptive list but rather as possibilities to consider.

1. **A focus on teaching and learning**

    A relentless focus on teaching and learning is, without question, a key characteristic of effective and improving schools in disadvantaged areas. Effective schools, in all contexts, tend to focus on academic achievement and improving instructional practices (Sharratt, 2018). Such schools succeed by introducing new teaching methods and improving the effectiveness of existing teaching methods.

    Evidence indicates that pupils from disadvantaged backgrounds benefit from large amounts of positive reinforcement from the teacher and respond well to being included and valued. Valuing pupils and making them feel part of the school family are important characteristics of effective and improving schools, along with an emphasis on student voice.

2. **Engaging parents and families**

As Chapter 5 will outline, creating positive relationships with parents/families and involving them in their children's education is one of the strongest indicators of lasting school improvement (Goodall, 2018a, 2018c; Harris & Goodall, 2008). Achieving this, however, is often difficult in socio-economically disadvantaged areas. Many parents or families may have experienced their own time in school negatively and, consequently, see little merit in formal education.

Some schools have successfully secured more parental/family engagement by providing parents/families with incentives to come to school, such as providing them with transportation or childcare. The evidence on parental/family engagement will be outlined in more detail in the next chapter, but the importance of involving parents/families in their children's education as early as possible cannot be overstated.

3. **Building a professional learning community**

One of the major findings from 30 years of research on school effectiveness is the fact that schools that improve, whatever their circumstance or context, do so by becoming a professional learning community (Harris, Jones, & Huffman, 2017). If improvement is to be secured and sustained, it is achieved through cultural change more so than structural change.

Professional learning communities are characterized by shared values and vision, collective responsibility for students' learning, reflective professional inquiry, collaboration, and the promotion of group as well as individual learning (Harris & Jones, 2010). In a professional learning community, there is authentic collaboration and staff are engaged in enquiry and reflection aimed at improving student learning outcomes. The school as a professional learning community is open to change and experimentation and is on a journey of continuous improvement.

As Chapter 6 will outline, teamwork and collaboration are crucial to building and maintaining a professional learning community. In a professional learning community, teachers talk with each other about teaching and learning, creating an inquisitive and change-oriented environment in which one innovation leads to another. In such schools, time is made available for common lesson planning and sharing of practice. Collective professionalism and joint enquiry are at the heart of building a functional and impactful professional learning community (Hargreaves & O'Connor, 2018).

4. **Investing in continuing professional learning**

A great deal has been written, promised, and delivered in the name of professional learning for teachers. The professional learning terrain is, without question, very busy and highly lucrative. Commercial providers, high-profile speakers, and glossy brochures fill this space with the tantalizing promise of school transformation, classroom improvement, and increased student performance (Improving Teaching, n.d.). "International surveys suggest that the average teacher spends 10.5 days per year engaged in courses, workshops, conferences, seminars, observation visits, or in-service training for the purposes of continuing professional development" (Sims & Fletcher-Wood, 2018, p. 1). How much of this makes a real, positive, and lasting difference to students' learning, however, remains questionable.

At the epicenter of any professional learning community is continuing professional learning that is authentic, inclusive, and impactful. Professional collaboration can be a catalyst for meaningful and transformative professional learning. Collaborative professional inquiry, informed by research, has been shown to be a key component in enhancing teacher quality and securing better learner outcomes.

Many of the models of professional collaboration and enquiry are research based; they emanate from empirical findings concerning organizational effectiveness. Collaborative professionalism reinforces the relationship between focused collaboration and high performance (Hargreaves & O'Connor, 2018). This collaborative way of working will be explored in more detail in Chapter 5.

5. **Creating a positive school culture**

Creating a positive school culture is one of the most widely cited elements in improving schools. High expectations are also important to student achievement, and this is particularly the case in schools serving a population with a low socioeconomic status. High expectations need to be transmitted to students, and this can be facilitated through monitoring of student work, positive feedback, and the setting of demanding but realistic student goals.

6. **Distributed leadership**

There have been countless studies over successive decades that have reached the same conclusion—leadership matters if lasting school improvement is the goal. There is no single example of an organizational turnaround or meltdown without leadership being intrinsically in the mix. All the above are unlikely to be achieved without effective leadership.

Evidence shows that leadership is "second only to the curriculum and teaching in its effect upon student learning" (Leithwood, Harris, & Hopkins, 2008, p. 4). In short, what leaders do makes a significant difference to organizational health, stability, and performance. Many studies have positively linked distributed leadership practice to improved student achievement outcomes, particularly for schools in difficulty (Harris, 2013).

Distributed leadership essentially means that those best equipped or skilled to lead do so in order to fulfill a goal or school requirement. Distributed leadership does not imply that everyone is a leader or that everyone leads but rather that those with the potential to lead at a given moment in time do so. It is a non-hierarchical, broad-based leadership practice that involves the many rather than the few (Harris, 2013).

In broad terms, leading for equity includes a set of leadership approaches aimed at addressing poor student achievement, which includes developing strategies to improve achievement, monitoring the impact of these strategies over time, and distributing leadership throughout the organization.

LEADING FOR EQUITY

Looking at the many books on leadership, there are many terms and descriptors for *leadership*. In fact, adjectival leadership abounds. This is when you put an adjective in front of the word *leadership* and claim a new idea or model. Hence, this section avoids the term *equity-focused leadership* and looks instead at *leading for equity.*

A recent study of effective leadership practices in schools that have improved their performance, despite being in difficult circumstances, suggests that leading for equity involves five key leadership practices (Harris et al., 2017, p. 12):

Figure 4.1 Five Key Practices in Leading for Equity

Source: Harris (2017).

The enactment of these practices will inevitably differ depending on the context, immediate need, or prevailing issues within the school. Each one will be explained briefly:

- *Expectations: Setting goals and new directions.* Much of the work on school improvement underlines the importance of the principal setting a new direction or pathway as a strong signal that change is about to happen (Leithwood, Harris, & Strauss, 2010). Essentially, their leadership is positioned as a point of departure from previous practice and performance.

- *Coordination: Managing different priorities.* The issue of competing priorities in turnaround schools is widely acknowledged. Most school leaders face a wide range of competing priorities and, in most cases, must balance conflicting agendas. Managing different priorities, therefore, is a critical dimension of leading for equity, as the management of different learner needs is imperative and important.

- *Integration of strategies and approaches.* The challenge for school leaders in schools in need of turnaround is exactly what to prioritize in the face of so many challenges and competing demands. Evidence suggests that leading for equity requires the careful sequencing and coordinating of improvement efforts so that all young people benefit.

- *Collaboration among staff and community.* Leadership for equity means building positive collaborative cultures in schools. This is done in a variety of ways that include getting buy-in from teachers and parents/families, getting support from the community, and gaining the trust of those within the school and outside it.

- *Enculturation: Harmony with cultural norms and expectations.* Effective leaders understand the context and the culture within which they work in order to mold their leadership decisions and practices accordingly. Contextually appropriate leadership is key in school improvement and school turnaround.

Many studies of school turnaround, particularly those from a Western perspective, tend to foreground the centrality of strategies or solutions for success. There is almost always a focus on the instrumental means to improvement, with relatively little consideration about how cultural factors affect the everyday lives of those who attend the school. Leading for equity means that working on the culture is far more important than making structural changes because, ultimately, it is the school culture that will bring sustained gains in student performance.

Leading for equity means that those in formal leadership roles often work in communities that are culturally different from their own. Many of them may not live in the community. Therefore, creating cultural harmony is a major task, as is ensuring that leadership actions fall within certain culturally accepted norms. Creating cultural harmony is a central feature of leading for equity, particularly within marginalized communities.

There are also a range of actions, behaviors, and priorities that leaders consistently demonstrate to secure better performance and outcomes. Research suggests that these include the following:

- Setting a goal and vision to generate a belief in a culture of improvement;
- Establishing clear expectations with students and staff and sharing a vision of improvement;
- A relentless focus on teaching and learning to generate a belief that all students have the capacity to learn and capability to learn;
- Setting of high standards and expectations for staff and students;
- Establishing clear expectations;
- Respecting others and imparting a sense of urgency for maintaining high academic standards;
- Exerting pressure upon staff and students to excel;
- Creating a positive school culture to foster a sense of community among staff and students;
- Involving the broader community in the work of the school; and
- Promoting continuous professional learning and development of staff to create a professional learning community as a school.

- Exercising flexible and distributed leadership to generate collective approaches to tackling highly complex problems, especially by investing in the leadership of others (Chapman & Harris, 2004)

Successful leadership in challenging circumstances is driven by a strong commitment to equity and an inherent sense of deep moral purpose. For some leaders, this moral purpose comes directly from the experience of growing up in similar circumstances and therefore feeling passionate about the need to make a difference to learners (Harris, 2010). For others, it is driven by a deep sense of social justice.

Leading for equity means putting the conditions in place for young people to achieve their potential, irrespective of background. Successful leaders in schools in challenging circumstances build collaboration, consensus, and community; they model compassionate but constructive leadership; they engage parents/families and stakeholders in transforming children's lives (Meyers & Smylie, 2017).

For such leaders, there are no guarantees of success; leading a school in difficulty is hard, relentless, and emotionally exhausting work. The leaders of such schools, as the evidence suggests, understand their context intimately and act in ways that are appropriate to the cultural and social expectations of the setting in which they work.

While there are generic leadership approaches that have been proven to work irrespective of setting (Leithwood et al., 2008), the fine-grained decision making that leaders undertake in challenging schools is inevitably and irrefutably context specific and context bound. The most successful leaders in these schools combine a personal passion with a deeply ingrained sense of social justice located within a profound understanding of context and a desire for equity.

They are leaders who personally relate to young people and families at risk, those who are vulnerable and need support. It is this relational quality, along with their compassion and caring, that mark these leaders out. Their compassion, passion, and determination to secure success for every child in every setting, even when facing the greatest odds, is their greatest asset and most powerful resource.

Schools, however, cannot tackle the net impact of poverty alone. The next chapter explores why working with families and the community is imperative if inequity is to be challenged and addressed.

CHAPTER
5

Leading Parental and Community Engagement

I was talking to a boy in year 7. He was already in a programme to prevent him from being excluded, and he was telling me that he was trying hard to behave well. I asked if his teachers were pleased with his progress. His answer summed up my area of research and has stayed with me—"Yeah, I guess it's nice when your teachers are happy but your dad's your dad!"—with a great deal of emphasis on the final word. Pleasing his teachers was okay but what motivated him, what was keeping him trying to behave, was his father's approval.

Janet Goodall (2018a)

Looking through a random selection of books on school improvement, you will find that leadership, professional learning, collaboration, and assessment for learning feature strongly. This is good news because it confirms that these are strategies or approaches that are worthwhile and can make a difference to a school and its performance. Looking at the indexes of many of these books, however, would lead you to conclude that parental and community engagement are, by comparison, relatively unimportant.

The impact of parents/families and the family environment on learner outcomes is significant and has gained greater status in both policy and practice (Goodall, 2017; Lepkowska & Nightingale, 2019). The rationale for parental/family engagement in their children's learning is simple and clear:

> We have a gap between the achievement of children from different backgrounds in this country, a gap which is appreciably larger than that in many other countries. Schools have gone some way to narrowing the gap but there remains more to be done. As I've argued for some time, the answer seems to lie outside of schools, as a very great deal of young people's achievement is determined outside the school gates. (Goodall, 2018b)

Disparities of family engagement in learning remain one of the most challenging and sensitive issues in education policy. Many policy makers have been wary of discussing the role that different parents/families play in their children's educational experience, much less finding ways to help parents/families offer better support to their children. That reticence has meant that educational inequalities and inequities harmful to individual children and society more widely have gone unchallenged.

Even when the role of parents/families and the family environment are in the scope of policy and research, there are challenging questions about disentangling the effect of family income and parents/families' qualifications from their engagement. It is too easy to implicitly criticize families who are already living in tough circumstances or to advocate measures that involve the government reaching too far into family life.

Notwithstanding such challenges, the evidence about the positive impact of parental/family engagement on learning and subsequent attainment remains compelling. Here is a brief overview of what we know:

- Parental/family engagement is a powerful lever for raising achievement and attainment in schools.

- Where parents/families and teachers work together to improve children's learning, the gains in achievement are significant.

- Parents/families have the greatest influence on the achievement of young people by supporting their learning in the home rather than supporting activities in the school. It is their support of learning within the home environment that makes the maximum difference in achievement.

- Many schools involve parents/families in school-based or school-related activities. This constitutes parental/family *involvement* rather than parental/family *engagement.*

- Parental/family engagement can encompass a whole range of activities with or within the school. Where these activities are not directly connected to learning, they have little impact on pupil achievement.

- Parental/family engagement is heavily linked to socioeconomic status as well as parental experience in education.

- Parents/families of certain ethnic and social groups are less likely to engage with the school. Schools that offer bespoke forms of support to these parents/families (i.e., literacy classes, parenting skill support) are more likely to engage them in their children's learning.

- Parental/family engagement is positively influenced by the child's level of attainment: the higher the level of attainment, the more parents/families get involved.

- Parental/family engagement is viewed as a good thing by teachers, parents/families, and students, although interpretations of the term vary.

- Students view parental/family engagement as being primarily about moral support and interest in their progress.

- Schools that successfully engage parents/families in learning consistently reinforce the fact that parents/families matter. They develop a two-way relationship with parents/families based on mutual trust, respect, and a commitment to improving learning outcomes.

- Parents/families who are viewed as "hard to reach" often see the school as hard to reach. The term is not useful or accurate; the important point is how the school reaches families and how families reach the school.

- Schools face certain barriers in engaging parents/families. These include practical issues, such as lack of time, language barriers, and childcare issues, and practical skills, such as literacy issues and the ability to understand and negotiate the school system.

All the above have a firm foundation in a great deal of international research evidence (e.g., Goodall, 2017; Harris, Andrew-Power, & Goodall, 2009; Morgan, 2016).

WHY PARENTS/FAMILIES MATTER

Young children whose parents read them five books a day enter kindergarten having heard about 1.4 million more words than children who are never read to (Grabmeier, 2019). Based on these calculations, by the time children are 5 years old, there are significant differences in word acquisition:

- Children who are never read to hear 4,662 words.
- Children who are read to 1–2 times per week hear 63,570 words.
- Children who are read to 3–5 times per week hear 169,520 words.
- Children who are read to daily hear 296,660 words.
- Children who are read five books a day hear 1,483,300 words.

The word gap of more than 1 million words between children raised in a literacy-rich environment and those who were never read to is striking. Children who hear more words are going to be better prepared to see those words in print when they enter school. This example shows the power of parental/family engagement in learning.

The importance of parents/families' educational attitudes and behaviors on children's educational attainment has also been well documented, especially in the developmental psychology literature. It shows that different elements of parents/families' educational attitudes and behaviors, such as the provision of a cognitively stimulating home environment, parental/family engagement in children's activities, and parental beliefs and aspirations, have been identified as having a significant effect on children's levels of educational achievement.

A great deal of contemporary research has reinforced a powerful association between parental/family engagement and student achievement. It highlights that parents/families' engagement in learning at home is far more significant than any other factor subjected to educational influence (Goodall, 2017, 2018a, 2018c; Goodall & Weston, 2018). The impact of parental/family engagement in learning activities in the home leads to better cognitive achievement, particularly in the early years.

In contrast, parental/family engagement (or, rather, *involvement*, which takes the form of in-school parental activity) has little effect on individual attainment. Put bluntly, parents/families volunteering in schools has little tangible contribution to academic attainment of individual students, although it is valuable for the schools and parents/families in terms of community relationships. There is an important difference between parents/families' involvement in schooling and parents/families' engagement with learning.

Parental/family engagement has an important effect on children's achievement and adjustment even after all other factors (such as social class, maternal education, and poverty) have been factored out. Among the non-school factors of school achievement, such as socioeconomic background, parents' educational attainment, family structure, ethnicity, and parental/family engagement, it is the latter that is the most strongly connected to attainment (Desforges & Abouchaar, 2003).

The impact of parental/family engagement arises from parental values and educational aspirations that are continuously exhibited through parental enthusiasm and positive parenting. While the effects of parental/family engagement, as they manifest in the home, can be significant, they are influenced by a wide range of factors. Disentangling the web of variables enmeshing the whole of family–school relationships and their impact on learning is daunting, and placing all the fragments of specific knowledge on the subject into a coherent framework is a real challenge. Yet levels of engagement and involvement vary considerably, depending on the parents/families and the context in which they find themselves.

BARRIERS TO PARENTAL/ FAMILY ENGAGEMENT

There are barriers to engaging parents/families in learning. For many parents/families who are deemed "hard to reach," the school is actually hard to reach. For many parents/families who failed at school, the school itself is an important and powerful barrier. Why would you want to return to a place where you failed? Consequently, communication with parents/families is pivotally important—so they know how much they matter and how they can make a difference to their child's educational progress.

Parental/family engagement is also strongly positively influenced by the child's level of attainment: the higher the level of attainment, the more parents/families are engaged. Parental expectations set the context within which young people develop and shape their own expectations and provide a framework within which decisions are made. There are, however, significant differences between parents/families in their level of involvement that are clearly associated with social class, poverty, and health and with parental perception of their role and their levels of confidence in fulfilling it.

Students from low socioeconomic families are more likely to be disaffected from school, as are students who attend schools that have a high percentage of students of low socioeconomic status (SES). As these risk factors compound, students from low SES families are even more likely to be dissatisfied and absent from school. This phenomenon of "double jeopardy" is also evident in analyses of student achievement: Low SES students who attend schools that predominantly serve low SES students are especially at risk of poor school performance because they have two factors working together.

Students are more likely to be engaged in school if they attend schools that have a high average SES, a strong disciplinary climate, good student–teacher relations, and high expectations for student success. Students from low SES backgrounds achieve more in schools where there are high SES students. In other words, peer groups and social mix affect outcomes and progress.

Parents/families' evenings are the usual way that schools engage parents/families, yet this is a particularly well-documented opportunity for creating parental frustration and confusion. While there is a broadly held desire among some parents/families for more involvement in schooling, there are clearly material (time and money) and psychological barriers that operate differently (and discriminatingly) across the social classes and individual differences among parents/families that operate within social classes. It remains the case, therefore, that middle-class parents/families are more involved in education and actively support their children's learning.

But how do you practically engage parents? What are the ways that work most effectively? Janet Goodall's new book, *100 Ideas for Primary Teachers: Engaging Parents* (Goodall & Weston, 2018) describes her top 10 practices for engaging parents:

1. Parents/families love their children and want the best for them. You, too, want the best for all of the children you work with. That's the basis of any engagement strategy—you're all working for the same goal.

2. Parents/families are at least as individual as the children in your class—what works for one child does not work for all, and the same is true of parents/families. To support them to engage with their children's learning, you need to get to know parents/families—what they want, what they need, and importantly, what they are already doing to support learning.

3. What's really important is that parents/families engage with children's learning—not that parents/families come to school. Some parents/families may never be able to come to school, for a whole host of reasons, but that doesn't mean they aren't or can't engage with learning or that they do not need support to do so.

4. Think about the barriers your parents/families face—these will be different for each cohort, each school, and sometimes each family. Do you know the bus schedules that allow parents to get to school? Do you know if they are working shifts, which makes it difficult for them to come to school? If they can't come, how else can you support them to support their children?

5. Parents/families know their children well, but differently than school staff do. It's very useful to ask the simple question, "What can you tell me about your child that will help me to help them learn?"

6. As educators, we know the difference between giving people information and having a dialogue with them. Schools are very good at giving parents/families information—and that's important—but it's not the same as having a dialogue—and it is having those dialogues that will build the relationships that will support children's learning.

7. Ensure that your website is easy to navigate for someone coming to it for the first time—and for someone using a phone to look at it. Having pictures of the classrooms can

be very useful (and reduce anxiety for visitors—parents, families, and new pupils!).

8. Let parents/families know what children will be learning and give them ideas about how to support that (e.g., "We're looking at fractions—talk about dividing a pizza or cake"; "We're looking at writing stories—talk to your child about what you like in a book or movie").

9. Consider meeting parents/families outside of school, particularly for parents who find it difficult to come into school. A leisure center, a local hall—wherever parents/families might be comfortable. Sometimes it's first steps like this that can lay the foundations of good relationships.

10. You already have many of the skills you need to support parents/families because you support learners all the time. Sometimes it's a matter of approaching interactions with parents as learning opportunities for parents, families, and education staff!

In terms of challenging inequality and inequity, more can be done to establish positive patterns of engagement between parents/families and teachers in order to set high expectations for learning. But engaging parents/families is only part of the solution to a multifaceted problem. Young people live within communities that shape their values and influence their behavior, so another way to directly reduce inequality and inequity is to reach out to the community.

ENGAGING THE COMMUNITY

As the long-term pattern of educational inequity looks set to remain, to rely on standard or standardized approaches to address this complex issue would seem both risky and unwise. There is evidence that improvements that have been secured through standardization are starting to plateau and the impact of the privatization of schooling in England (academies) and in the United States (charter schools) are not bringing the investment returns that were anticipated. Evaluation data, however, show rather mixed results.

The Center for Research on Education Outcomes (CREDO, 2009) found mildly negative effects of charter schools relative to traditional state schools. Other research, which has indicated more positive outcomes, underlines that these relative gains remain quite modest (CfBT, 2012). The cracks are starting to appear in the United States, and accusations of the misuse and misappropriation of public funding abound (Ravitch, 2020). In short, the marketization of education and privatization has resulted in many schools in the most difficult contexts becoming less able to raise performance levels.

A combination of market individualism and control through constant and comparative assessments (national and international) has demoted certain schools, in certain contexts, to the lower echelons of performance indefinitely. As Michael Apple (2001) explains,

> In marketized plans, more affluent parents/families often have more flexible hours and can visit multiple schools. They have cars—often more than one—and can afford to drive their children across town to attend a "better school." They can as well provide the hidden cultural resources such as camps and after school programs that give their children an "ease," a "style" that seems "natural" and acts as a set of cultural resources. (p. 73)

As noted earlier, parents/families in poor and disadvantaged communities are less able to work the system, leaving more and more children to re-experience the same cycle of underachievement. The attainment gap between the richest and poorest in society is as great as it was 20 years ago. Social class, ethnicity, race, and gender differences continue to haunt education systems. In terms of tackling inequity, education policy continues to have made very little headway and relatively little difference.

The reason for this lack of substantive change is partly to be blamed on the complexity and scale of the issue. It is also to be blamed on the naivete of policy interventions that are fragmented, piecemeal, and top down. An alternative solution, therefore, is to start with the community and to introduce targeted resources and integrated forms of support that allow schools and their communities to generate and sustain improvements on their terms, in their context. Community schools that offer integrated services are also one effective way of reducing the effects and outcomes of inequity. For example,

> Cities like New York City, Baltimore, and Oakland . . . are making both systemic commitments and intentional investments to ensure that neighborhood school communities serve as hubs for high-quality instruction and for the supports children and families need to break down barriers to achievement. Schools in these districts are partnering and coordinating with dozens of nonprofits, government agencies, community associations, direct service agencies, and corporations to battle chronic community issues, identified in community-inclusive needs assessments.

> At West Baltimore's Robert Coleman Elementary School, one of the nearly 80 partnerships funded with dollars allocated by Baltimore City via the Family League of Baltimore is with a meditation nonprofit called the Holistic Life Foundation. When students have conflicts in the classroom or with each other, the school has students engage in 15-minute "mindfulness moments." The innovative blend of meditation and yoga that the foundation developed encourages calming down, processing feelings, admitting mistakes, and restoring good faith. . . .

> For their children to access the dozens of programs and services on offer, parents are required to volunteer at least two hours a month at their schools.

> Baltimore is beginning to see the results from these coordinated efforts. Students are happier, families are more engaged, attendance is rising, and truancy has fallen, giving students

and teachers the ability to focus on what matters: achievement. Citywide, chronic neighborhood issues—hunger, mental and physical health, unemployment, and youth enrichment—are all being addressed inside school buildings and through food pantries and feeding programs, school-based health clinics, parent resource centers, out-of-school programming, and other innovative partnerships and initiatives. In fiscal year 2012, Baltimore funded 18 community schools around the city. As of fiscal year 2016, the city had tripled its number of funded community schools to 56. (Batchelor & Wattenberg, 2017)

But how do schools engage and connect with a highly diverse community? Here is one example:

Merrylands High School (MHS) has 800 students from 55 cultural backgrounds. Of the students, 82% are from non-English-speaking backgrounds. This includes 17 Aboriginal students (2.3%) and 77 refugee students (10%).

Arabic, Turkish, Afghani, Hindi, and Pacific Islander (Maori, Tongan, and Samoan) are the most common languages other than English. The community is a low socioeconomic area. It had dropping enrollments, poor student engagement, a reputation for violence, and poor community confidence.

The principal realized that engaging with the school community was the key to raising attainment. The school and the community started to work together to co-design high-impact practices that resulted in a significant improvement in outcomes. Most notable were 5-year trend data of Higher School Certificate (HSC) achievements, which have seen unprecedented HSC successes and university entrance rates.

Organization, legacy programs, and administrative practices that shackled progressive and innovative thinking and practices were removed from the school. Instead, a relentless focus was placed on teaching and learning, aspirations, opportunities, exciting possibilities, and multiple entry and engagement points for learners, educators, and the community. Inclusivity and meeting the learning needs of individuals replaced the previous and well-worn focus of well-being and disadvantage.

Administrative and welfare roles within the school were replaced by teaching/learning roles with clear responsibilities, including the development of individual learning plans for *every* student. Students were encouraged to become experts in their own learning.

Strong home, school, and community partnerships replaced combative and distrusting relationships. This included schools delivering goal-setting programs at school camp, presenting school development day programs at school on cultural under-standings and keynote presentations at State Premier Forums, hosting school events, participating in learning with up to three generations (and translators) in school classes, and attending university in situ—all designed for greater understanding.

The focus on pedagogy, empowerment, agency, and inclusivity soon paid dividends for students:

- Justice came to Australia as a 17-year-old refugee with-out family of any description and often had home utilities cut off, but through a personalized learning program that was appropriately resourced, his life experience possibil-ities and opportunities were enhanced. Justice went to Technical and Further Education (TAFE) and completed a Certificate IV. He is now gainfully and happily employed.

- David is legally blind and had a mother who was severely debilitated by substance abuse. His education was fre-quently broken and as a 12-year-old, he experienced sig-nificant life trauma most of us cannot imagine. He has now completed his degree in teaching.

- Angela is a non-English-speaking background (NESB) student who worked hard throughout school but often needed to access additional support, especially in her senior year. She is now at university (for industrial design) and is working as a paraprofessional at the school to sup-port others.

(Continued)

(Continued)

These are three examples of life-changing opportunities that resulted from the school's commitment to equity. Many refugee students are pursuing tertiary education. Proud parents, family, or caregivers speak of never imagining such a possibility for their children. The MHS school community worked intelligently, compassionately, and strategically to afford the young people in the school access to a quality education. The community continues to engage with and support the school.

Lila Mularczyk
Principal
Order of Australia Medal (OAM)

Looking at this school example and many others that reflect community-based support suggests an integrated model of community engagement. This has four dimensions:

- Context-specific support and program differentiation;
- Specialist and expert support (i.e., mental health services, counseling);
- Parental/family buy-in and engagement; and
- Inclusive access.

When community resources are used to strengthen schools, families, and student learning, then positive outcomes can arise. In his book *Failure Is Not an Option*, Alan Blankstein (2012) offers a few practical ways in which community engagement can be fostered and led:

1. Developing partnerships with local businesses and service groups to advance student learning and to assist schools and families;

2. Encouraging employers to adopt policies and practices that support and promote adult participation in children's education; and

3. Collaborating with community agencies to provide family support services and adult learning opportunities, enabling parents/families to more fully participate in activities that support education.

These approaches locate the community at the heart of the real work of regeneration, renewal, and reconfiguration. They are premised on the central idea that schools are more likely to be effective if they reach out and work with their immediate community networks, and that includes other schools and parents/families.

To move to a community-based model of improvement that tackles inequity head-on at a local level will require policy commitment, extra funding, and specialist support. Raising standards of achievement for the many rather than the few can only be secured by a form of local governance that represents and acts upon the voices of those living and learning in the local community.

Integrated community provision works best when the school is at the heart of the provision and when it provides a range of services and access points to the local community. Community engagement is a reciprocal and democratic relationship where the ebb and flow of services, people, and resources are closely configured to the needs of the school and the community. This is enhanced through authentic and focused professional collaboration.

The next chapter proposes that collective responsibility, collaborative support, and cross-community engagement is a powerful model of school improvement rather than that premised on savage and ruthless competition between schools.

CHAPTER
6

Leading Professional Collaboration

I wonder how many children's lives might be saved if we educators disclosed what we know to each other.

Roland Barth (2001, p. 60)

Parent and community engagement are essentially about building a learning community within and outside the school. Professional collaboration within and between schools, as the quote above showed, can be a potent lever for greater equity as teachers strive to work together to overcome the barriers to learning that many children face.

We know a great deal about how collective engagement and collaborative work can address common problems and build a cohesive and respectful community. Using data to inform improvement is now a generally accepted practice, as is the need to consider the individual learning needs of children who come from diverse settings and backgrounds (Sharratt, 2018).

Around the globe every year, teachers routinely engage in hundreds of hours of professional development and training associated with contractual responsibilities rather than a professional entitlement or right. Much of what passes as professional learning or training, however, often takes the form of courses that teachers must attend. The quality and delivery of this training can vary considerably, and generally, its impact is questionable.

In contrast, focused teacher inquiry and professional collaboration can make a positive difference to student learning (Harris, Jones, & Huffman, 2017; Timperley, Wilson, Barrar, & Fung, 2007). For professional learning communities, enquiry networks and lesson studies have an extensive and strong empirical base. Professional learning communities have been shown to be one of the most powerful forms of collective inquiry within, between, and across schools (Harris & Jones, 2017; Vescio, Ross, & Adams, 2008).

As highlighted earlier in this book, professional learning communities (PLCs) within schools are strongly correlated to a school's effectiveness, along with a collaborative and cohesive culture. Consequently, PLCs have become a common approach to teacher collaboration in the pursuit of school improvement and improving student attainment. There is now significant international literature on this topic (Harris et al., 2017) that underlines the benefits of teacher collaboration by being in a professional community in terms of improvements in learning and teaching.

The penultimate chapter of this book, therefore, looks at how collaboration within and between schools can be a powerful force for tackling inequities and inequalities. Teachers working together to address specific learning issues that children face and to address them collectively is a powerful intervention that leads to positive results. Teacher collaboration, however, can take many forms, and there is not only one model to follow.

PROFESSIONAL COLLABORATION WITH IMPACT?

The quality of teaching is by far the most important school-based determinant of pupils' educational attainment and educational success. It remains the case that pupils make less progress when they have a teacher who does not have a formal teaching qualification, is newly qualified, is less experienced, and is without a degree in the relevant subject, and when teacher turnover at their school is high. Engaging teachers in research and inquiry as part of a process of high-quality professional learning can be a contributor to improving their practice (Cordingley, 2015).

Campbell and her team (2016) underline how collaborative professional learning is a key component in raising teacher quality and securing better learner outcomes. This work reinforces that professional learning must be focused, rigorous, and purposeful to make any real or lasting difference to professional practice and student learning outcomes. To be most effective, professional collaborative inquiry within, across, and between schools should be systematic and focused on improving learning and teaching (Sharratt & Planche, 2016).

The professional learning arena, however, is overcrowded with advice, ready-made solutions, and models of collaborative inquiry that simply have little or no substantive evidential base. While there may be nothing intrinsically wrong with adopting or adapting models of collaborative inquiry that do not emanate from a strong research position, it could explain why evidence of impact, in the form of better learning outcomes for students, may not always be forthcoming from teachers' collaborative engagement.

Hattie (2015) proposes, "There is no way that a system will make an overall difference to student achievement by working one teacher at a time" (p. 5); this collaboration has to be purposeful and focused. It is proposed in this chapter that collaborative inquiry can only be focused, purposeful, and impactful within a clear model or framework that encompasses and incorporates evaluative measures from the outset.

There are several potential reasons to explain this disconnect between teachers' collaborative inquiry and a positive impact on student learning outcomes. The first of these concerns focuses on the transferability of knowledge and the generally held assumption that the knowledge or skills developed through professional learning programs can be automatically applied to the classroom. Several decades ago, Joyce and Showers (1981) explained this as the problem of transfer from the "workshop to the workplace"; they essentially argued that training or development conducted outside the teacher's workplace made the possibility of transfer highly problematic.

A second reason for the potential disconnects between teachers' collaborative inquiry and an impact on students' learning could be related to the mode of collaboration itself and, by association, the way professional collaboration is enacted. For example, Hargreaves and Dawe (1990) talk about "contrived collegiality" and how, if poorly formulated, professional collaboration in the form of PLCs can dissolve into little more than superficial engagement. The main message is that even though the literature on collaborative inquiry presupposes that teachers' collective work is positive and empowering, if weakly constructed and realized, it can prove to be little more than groupthink and low-level consensus.

A third reason resides in the fact that, for many teachers, external training or professional development events are experienced individually. As noted earlier, most teachers attend courses independently in their subject area or on a topic of relevance or interest to them. Even though there may be some expectation that they will share or cascade the knowledge gained on their return to school, this rarely happens. While the routine sharing of information and knowledge is perfectly possible, sharing the actual learning experience is not. Consequently, the learning gained from professional training courses and events remains of benefit to the individual only, and the return on this investment for other staff remains negligible or nonexistent.

Finally, in many professional development courses and training sessions, the evaluation mechanisms that are deployed strongly signal that the learning is about the teacher and not the student. Typically, after professional training sessions, teachers are asked to fill out an evaluation form or to engage in some form of follow-up interview. Even if they are asked to outline how their new learning will be used to change and improve student learning, this is rarely followed up or verified in any way. Clearly, teacher learning is important, but if it fails to impact upon student learning in some positive or tangible way, then the exact purpose of that professional learning and development needs to be questioned (Harris & Jones, 2010).

Three things are clear:

1. When teachers are part of a functioning PLC, they are more reflective on their professional practice and more willing to innovate in the classroom;
2. Under the right conditions, a PLC can build professional capacity and professional capital; and
3. An authentic PLC can have a positive impact on learner outcomes.

PROFESSIONAL LEARNING COMMUNITIES

So much has already been written about PLCs in so many different ways that there is much confusion about PLCs today. As DuFour (2004) notes, "The term has been used so ubiquitously that it is in danger of losing all meaning." Hence, it is important to be crystal clear at the outset. Essentially, what constitutes a PLC can be understood in three very different but overlapping ways:

- Firstly, there is the *whole-school* interpretation, where the entire school is considered to be operating as a PLC by adhering to certain shared norms and values;
- Secondly, there is a *within-school* interpretation, where collaborative teams or groups take responsibility for leading research, improvement, and innovation; and

- Thirdly, there is an *across-school* interpretation, where the collaborative activity between teachers occurs in a school-to-school environment, embodying and reflecting network learning.

Central to the purpose of PLCs is an improvement of teaching practices and a focus on professional development aimed ultimately at providing the best learning opportunities for students. Lieberman and Mace (2009) suggest that teachers will be more likely to collaborate around the purpose of improving teaching when their current knowledge and instructional practices are valued and utilized as a foundation.

Despite a great deal of enthusiasm for PLCs among practitioners, much of the writing points to the positive aspects of PLCs and tends to overlook issues of conflict or dissent that can emerge when teachers work together. Some have warned that PLCs can sometimes turn into "professional sects" that operate in ways that are conducive to consensus rather than to critique or challenge (Hargreaves, 2007).

So, when PLCs are aimed at improving equity, what do they reflect?

- *Shared focus.* Clarity about purpose is at the heart of effective collaboration (Sharratt, 2018). Many PLCs focus explicitly on equity issues and are keen to close the gaps in attainment between different groups of children.
- *Product, not process.* This process is one that leads to some outcome or impact that directly benefits learners. When PLCs start and end with student data, there is a smaller chance of PLCs being process driven and devoid of content.
- *Active enquiry.* Effective PLCs have enquiry at their core: Teachers are actively researching and collectively learning to solve a problem or tackle an issue that students face.
- *Student data.* Effective PLCs start and end with student data; in this way, impact on learners can be gauged.
- *Not consensus.* While PLCs are initially based on cooperation among teachers, they include within them the possibility of challenge and dissonance as teachers work with each other to achieve new understandings of learning and new ways of working.

While the nature, focus, and manifestation of PLCs inevitably vary from context to context, there are three questions or tests to bear in mind:

1. Is the PLC work being implemented at a superficial or deep level?
2. Is there evidence of impact on students, teachers, and the school system?
3. To what extent is the PLC work focused on equity issues?

While a great deal of work takes place within and across schools every day under the label of PLCs, these three tests—*implementation, impact,* and *sustainability*—provide a basis for distinguishing between well-meaning, worthy, cooperative work and impactful professional collaborative activity that has equity issues at the core.

In terms of professional collaboration for equity, there are seven tests that should be applied:

1. Is the professional collaborative learning premised upon clear intentions, transparent ways of working, and a shared rationale of equity for the joint work? (clarity of focus)
2. Does the professional collaborative learning necessitate continuous engagement with student data to inform all stages in the process of interdependent learning? (consistent use of student data)
3. Is the professional collaborative learning more than cooperation? Is it collaboration that is disciplined and focused on equity issues? (collaboration with purpose)
4. Are there regular updates to other staff about progress and a clear focus on the impact on students? (communication and dissemination)
5. Is the professional collaborative learning engaging the expertise, skill, and knowledge of those within the group or team to support changes that result in greater equity? (capacity building and engagement)
6. How far is the professional collaborative learning focused on systematic enquiry and reflection that can secure positive changes in equity outcomes? (coherent and consistent action)

7. Has the professional collaborative learning secured positive changes in student learning and equity? (evaluating outcomes)

These tests provide a checklist for those engaged in collaborative ways of learning that foster more equitable outcomes. They are not the only list, but they are derived from working with teachers who are attempting to tackle equity issues in a variety of different countries and settings.

But how do we ensure that equity issues are at the heart of professional collaboration? In answering this question, Ainscow (2016) proposes three interlinked areas in which equity issues can be more fully explored:

- *Within schools.* These are issues that arise from school and teacher practices. They include the ways in which students are taught and engage with their learning; the ways in which teaching groups are organized and the different kinds of opportunities that result from this organization; the kinds of social relationships and personal support that are characteristic of the school; the ways in which the school responds to diversity in terms of attainment, gender, ethnicity, and social background; and the kinds of relationships the school builds with families and local communities.

- *Between schools.* These are issues that arise from the characteristics of local school systems. They include the ways in which different types of schools emerge locally; the ways in which these schools acquire different statuses and that hierarchies emerge in terms of performance and preference; the ways in which schools compete or collaborate; the processes of integration and segregation that concentrate students with similar backgrounds in different schools; the distribution of educational opportunities across schools; and the extent to which students in every school can access similar opportunities.

- *Beyond schools.* This far-reaching arena includes the wider policy context within which schools operate; the family processes and resources that shape how children learn and develop; the interests and understandings of the professionals working in schools; and the demographics, economics, cultures, and histories of the areas served by schools. It also includes the underlying social and economic processes at national and—in many respects—global levels out of which local conditions arise.

Professional collaboration has the potential to support efforts to improve equity at the school level, but only if it is focused, purposeful, and authentic. Similar to all the micro-level strategies outlined in this book, it is fully acknowledged that professional collaboration can only narrow the equity gap so far. As Basis Bernstein (2003) said, "Schools cannot compensate for society."

The last chapter, therefore, returns to the main argument of this book—tackling equity requires deep structural and societal change.

CHAPTER
7

Reflections and Alternatives

Leading is difficult. It can upset the status quo and entrenched interests, so don't expect it to be easy. Reminding education leaders to consider the interests of children ahead of those of adults, especially if you are proposing a system recall, implies a disruptive change to the way adults operate.

Professor Adrian Piccoli, Gonski Institute,
University of South Wales

The real "results" of education are in the child's heart and mind and soul, beyond the reach of any tape or measuring machine.

Edmond Holmes (1911)

The pervasive and narrowly formulated understanding of what works is now limiting the system's capacity for equitable development.

Kirsten Kerr and Mel Ainscow (2017, p. 12)

nequity is a social failure, pure and simple. It guarantees better outcomes for some and not for others. As the chapters in this book have outlined, leadership for equity is most visible in highly deprived communities and the schools that serve them. It is here that the hardest educational work gets done and where effective leadership and teaching are so critically important.

Leaders of the most challenging schools are passionate and driven. They know that building strong communities within and across schools is part of the solution, as is engaging parents/families more in their children's learning. They also know that there are no simple remedies but that linking with the wider community to find mutual solutions is important, as is building a strong infrastructure of support around the child that includes attention to well-being and mental health support.

Leadership for equity is determined but fair, distributed but purposeful, and inherently morally driven. The leaders who work in our most challenging schools and communities deeply care about the young people who learn and live there. This sort of leadership cannot be taught; it cannot be packaged into a training course; it cannot be summarized into neat checklists. Leadership for equity is lived out in the daily work of being an educator first and a leader second.

It is not a job for the fainthearted or for those more concerned with climbing their own personal career ladder. These leaders know the harsh reality of inadequate funding, of limited resources, and of teacher shortages and how families are adversely affected by changes in their personal circumstances.

As argued at the start of this book, the macro influences of poverty, inequality, corruption, and politics are the main reasons why inequity thrives and survives. So, we must be realistic; we cannot simply eradicate overnight the forces that fuel and perpetuate cycles of inequity. Those who enjoy privilege and power are unlikely to sacrifice this anytime soon.

You only need to look at some of the current political leaders on the world stage to see that this is true. Hence, the small, practical, micro steps and day-by-day actions by those leading communities, schools, and classrooms will have to suffice while the larger ambition of a fair and equitable society is pursued.

The final section of this book revisits some of its big messages and highlights what needs to be done if equity is to truly be at the heart of political, social, and educational reform.

MORE FUNDING

The challenges of growing up in a poor household, society, or country have never been so clear or troubling. In April 2019, a survey (Burns, 2019) of more than 8,600 National Education Union (NEU) members from across the United Kingdom found that an overwhelming 91% said that poverty was a factor in limiting children's capacity to learn, with almost half (49%) deeming it a major factor. Among state schoolteachers, the figures rose to 97% and 52%. Overall, half the teachers who responded said pupil poverty in 2019 was worse than in 2016. Poverty is not necessarily confined to families where no one works; it also affects homes with parents/families who are working low-paid jobs but are still not able to afford the basics. One teacher commented, "The ones who are in crisis are not only the children whose parents/families do not work, but the ones who do."

Schools that serve populations of children who come from poor or disadvantaged settings generally do the very best they can to offset the worst effects of poverty on educational attainment. They try as far as possible to mitigate the impact of inequity on educational outcomes. Yet funding cuts to schools in need mean that hard choices must be made, such as cutting breakfast clubs or mental health support for young people, which can have a profound and devastating effect: "While a proportion of parents use breakfast clubs because working hours make it difficult to feed their children at home, more and more schools are reporting that the service is being used by families unable to afford enough food" (Rayner, 2012).

The return on the investment in better funding to schools is economically and socially significant. A report from the Gonski

Institute for Education (Holden & Zhang, n.d.) at University of New South Wales (UNSW) Sydney has calculated that Australia could add more than $50 billion to its annual gross domestic product (GDP) by improving educational outcomes for students in regional, rural, and remote areas of the country. It states,

> If the human capital gap between urban and non-urban Australia was closed, Australia's GDP could be increased by 3.3%, or $56 billion. To put this in perspective, this is larger than the contribution of the entire Australian tourism industry. Put another way, one would need to quadruple the size of the Australian beef industry to achieve the same economic improvement.
>
> Yet these are only the direct effects, on wages, of closing the human capital gap. There are important spillovers in addition to this, such as improvements in physical and mental health and enrichment of communities. . . . Furthermore, there is a multiplier effect throughout the economy from increased productivity and wages which we do not include. Thus, the size of the benefits we identify are in many ways quite conservative. (p. 4)

This is a powerful endorsement that equity has significant economic and social benefits. With such a clear rationale and justification, why is it that we keep seeking simpler solutions from other systems?

NO SIMPLE SOLUTIONS

In the past 10 years, the education policy landscape has changed dramatically, but the core challenges faced by local teachers and leaders have changed little. Most are still struggling to square the demands for increasing excellence, understood in the narrowest of terms, with the realities of children's lives outside of school. The pressure to embed new policies and practices is so relentless that it can detract from asking key questions about what education reforms are needed to achieve or create a more equitable system.

This book commenced with the idea that many of our current approaches to measuring excellence in education exacerbate inequity. In an alternative future, the idea of excellence *through* equity would prevail, along with the recognition that a more equitable society is a more educated society.

Instead of looking for simple solutions to the latest round of educational problems, the consistent effort to tackle inequity and inequality would be the core way of raising educational performance and standards. Rather than have equity follow as the poor relation of excellence, reform efforts would be centrally focused on securing and maintaining greater equity throughout the system.

One major implication of this alternative future would be to walk away from the "big tests," or the large-scale international assessments, and to move toward small or smaller data (Sahlberg, 2018). Unquestionably, this would require a great deal of political bravery because there is almost a global compulsion for countries to participate. The net result of withdrawing or downgrading the importance of these tests would be to focus on what matters most in education in context and to open up a discussion about core educational values rather than chasing Program for International Student Assessment (PISA) rankings (Breakspear, 2016).

But how high does the tide have to get before those who are leading education systems realize that the big tests are simply not meant to guide the fine-grained decisions that educators make in classrooms every day, which are so important? Within schools, teachers, support staff, and school leaders work with intricate small data that guide professional judgment and actions. This judgment emanates from deep professional knowledge and understanding. Small data allow teachers to make important and influential instructional decisions in their classrooms (Sharratt, 2018). Knowing that Shanghai does well in PISA is not that helpful when teaching mathematics or English to learners with diverse needs.

WITHIN-SYSTEM LEARNING

National policy makers have become so obsessed and immersed in the "what works" tidal wave that they have forgotten to consider the experience, wisdom, and knowledge held *within* the system itself. Introducing new strategies or temporary interventions that work elsewhere simply does not work in the long term.

There are no easy answers to inequity, but the solution does not reside in fleeting projects, borrowed initiatives, or piecemeal solutions. Time and time again, these do not live up to expectations. Conversely, as this book has argued throughout its pages, leading for equity and excellence requires a significant shift in policy thinking and a radical departure from a position in which some students are destined to succeed and others are destined to fail.

A more equitable education system cannot only be concerned with a narrowly defined set of measures or standards. A far broader vision is needed that focuses on the purposes of education, and alternative forms of accountability are needed to reflect what is valued rather than what is easily measured. A more equitable education system will need to address the real barriers to opportunity for all students, most of which occur beyond the school walls.

We cannot magically wipe the slate clean and simply start over. This is not an option. It is possible, however, that structural change at scale can occur where the policy purpose, ambition, and commitment are unequivocally focused on equity first and excellence second. Governments can support a mature debate about the broader aims and purposes of education and its underpinning values. Policy makers can unlock the hold of the Organization for Economic Cooperation and Development (OECD) on its education systems and define their own version of excellence; they just need to be brave enough to do so.

Policy makers also need to listen far more to those within the education systems, to the professionals who are so often excluded from substantive policy debates and decisions. They need to hear the voices of those teachers, leaders, and support staff on the front lines who are dealing with the brutal and heart-wrenching consequences of inequity and inequality. These education professionals are the true leaders of equity and excellence.

We leave the final words of this book to a great educator, a good friend, and a real champion of social justice:

The cost of educational failure has become too expensive. We cannot just sit on the sidelines anymore. Equity is a moral imperative.

Professor Sam Stringfield (1949–2016)

Now is the time to step off the sidelines.

References

Ainscow, M. (2016). Collaboration as a strategy for promoting equity in education: Possibilities and barriers. *Journal of Professional Capital and Community*, *1*(2), 159–172. Retrieved from https://doi.org/10.1108/JPCC-12-2015-0013

Alexander, R. J. (2012). Moral panic, miracle cures and educational policy: What can we really learn from international comparison? *Scottish Educational Review*, 4–21.

Andrews, J., & Perera, N. (2017, December 21). Access to high performing schools in England. *Education Policy Institute*. Retrieved from https://epi.org.uk/wp-content/uploads/2017/12/Access-to-high-performing-schools_EPI_.pdf

Apple, M. W. (2001). Comparing neo-liberal projects and inequality in education. *Comparative Education*, *37*(4), 409–423.

Baker, J. (2019a, March 10). "On its last legs": Why the world is abandoning NAPLAN-style tests. *The Sydney Morning Herald*. Retrieved from https://www.smh.com.au/education/on-its-last-legs-why-the-world-is-abandoning-naplan-style-tests-20190308-p512v4.html?ref=rss&utm_medium=rss&utm_source=rss_feed

Baker, J. (2019b, April 12). "People are frightened of NAPLAN": Australia's testing dilemma. *The Sydney Morning Herald*. Retrieved from https://www.smh.com.au/education/people-are-frightened-of-naplan-australia-s-testing-dilemma-20190411-p51dcu.html

Baroutsis, A., & Lingard, B. (2017). Counting and comparing school performance: An analysis of media coverage of PISA in Australia, 2000–2014. *Journal of Education Policy*, *32*(4), 432–449. doi:10.1080/02680939.2016.1252856

Baroutsis, A., & Lingard, B. (2018, February 19). PISA-shock: How we are sold the idea our PISA rankings are shocking and the damage it is doing to schooling in Australia. *EduResearch Matters*. Retrieved from https://www.aare.edu.au/blog/?p=2714

Barrett, D., & Zapotosky, M. (2019, March 12). FBI accuses wealthy parents including celebrities in college entrance bribery scheme. *The Washington Post*. Retrieved from https://www.washingtonpost.com/world/national-security/fbi-accuses-wealthy-parents-including-celebrities-in-college-entrance-bribery-scheme/2019/03/12/d91c9942-44d1-11e9-8aab-95b8d80a1e4f_story.html

Barth, R. S. (2001). Teacher leader. *Phi Delta Kappan, 82*(6), 443–449.

Batchelor, M., & Wattenberg, R. (2017, August 3). A memo to the D.C. public schools chancellor. *Washington City Paper*. Retrieved from https://www.washingtoncitypaper.com/news/article/20971334/a-memo-to-the-dc-public-schools-chancellor

Bazelais, P., Lemay, D. J., Doleck, T., Hu, X. S., Vu, A., & Yao, J. (2018). Grit, mindset, and academic performance: A study of pre-university science students. *EURASIA Journal of Mathematics, Science and Technology Education, 14*, 12.

Bennett, N. (2001). *Corruption in education systems in developing countries: What it is doing to the young*. Retrieved from http://iacconference.org/documents/10th_iacc_workshop_Corruption_in_Education_Systems_in_Developing_Countries.pdf

Benns, R. (2017). *Avis Glaze: The children cannot wait*. Victoria, BC, Canada: Friesen Press.

Bernstein, B. B. (2003). *Class, codes and control: Applied studies towards a sociology of language* (Vol. 2). New York, NY: Psychology Press.

Blankstein, A. M. (2012). *Failure is not an option* (3rd ed.). Thousand Oaks, CA: Corwin.

Bray, M., & Lykins, C. (2012). *Shadow education: Private supplementary tutoring and its implications for policy makers in Asia* (No. 9). Asian Development Bank.

Breakspear, S. L. (2016). *Measuring how the world learns: An examination of the OECD's PISA and its uses in national system evaluation* (Doctoral dissertation). University of Cambridge, Cambridge, England.

Breakspear, S. L., Peterson, A., Alfadala, A., & Khair, M. S. B. (2017). Developing agile leaders of learning: School leadership policy for dynamic times. *World Summit for Education*.

Bridge. (n.d.). Bridge believes every child has the right to high quality education and works in partnership with governments, parents and teachers to ensure access to quality education. *Bridge International Academies*. Retrieved from https://www.bridgeinternationalacademies.com/

Brown, P., Lauder, H., & Ashton, D. (2010). *The global auction: The broken promises of education, jobs and incomes*. Oxford, England: Oxford University Press.

Burdett, N., & O'Donnell, S. (2016). Lost in translation? The challenges of educational policy borrowing. *Educational Research, 58*(2), 113–120. doi: 10.1080/00131881.2016.1168678

Burns, J. (2012). How should heads handle inadequate teachers? *BBC News.* Retrieved from https://www.bbc.com/news/education-16547703

Burns, J. (2019, April 14). Worsening child poverty harms learning, say teachers. *BBC News.* Retrieved from https://www.bbc.co.uk/news/education-47902642?intlink_from_url=https://www.bbc.co.uk/news/topics/clm164grwrrt/child-poverty&link_location=live-reporting-story

Campbell, C., Lieberman, A., & Yashkina, A. (2016). Developing professional capital in policy and practice: Ontario's teacher learning and leadership program. *Journal of Professional Capital and Community, 1*(3), 219–236.

Carragher, A. (2018, December 14). What states with the worst teacher shortages are doing to entice teachers to relocate. *teachaway.* Retrieved from https://www.teachaway.com/blog/states-with-teacher-shortages

Center for Research on Education Outcomes (CREDO). (2009). *Multiple choice: Charter school performance in 16 states.* Retrieved from https://credo.stanford.edu/reports/MULTIPLE_CHOICE_CREDO.pdf

CfBT. (2012). *Impact evaluation of private sector involvement in education.* Retrieved from http://documents.worldbank.org/curated/en/325281468161085236/pdf/665860WP00PUBL0ct0evaluation0report.pdf

Chapman, C. (2019). Using research to promote equity within education systems: Possibilities and barriers. *British Educational Research Journal.*

Chapman, C., & Harris, A. (2004). Improving schools in difficult and challenging contexts: Strategies for improvement. *Educational Research, 46*(3), 219–228.

Chapman, C., Muijs, D., Reynolds, D., Sammons, P., & Teddlie, C. (Eds.). (2016). *The Routledge international handbook of educational effectiveness and improvement.* New York, NY: Routledge.

Childress, S. M., Doyle, D. P., & Thomas, D. A. (2009). *Leading for equity: The pursuit of excellence in the Montgomery County public schools.* Cambridge, MA: Harvard Education Press.

Chu, L. (2017). *Little soldiers: An American boy, a Chinese school and the global race to achieve.* London, England: Hachette UK.

Clegg, N., Allen, R., Fernandes, S., Freedman, S., & Kinnock, S. (2017, July 13). *Commission on inequality in education.* London, England: Social Market Foundation. Retrieved from http://www.smf.co.uk/publications/commission-inequality-education/

Cook, H. (2019, April 3). Mental illness the hidden drag on children's grades. *The Age.* Retrieved from https://www.theage.com.au/national/victoria/

mental-illness-the-hidden-drag-on-children-s-grades-20190403-p51ahd.html

Cordingley, P. (2015). The contribution of research to teachers' professional learning and development. *Oxford Review of Education, 41*(2), 234–252.

Coughlan, S. (2018, January 24). England and US will not take PISA tests in tolerance. *BBC News*. Retrieved from https://www.bbc.co.uk/news/business-42781376

Darling-Hammond, L. (2007). Third annual Brown lecture in education research—The flat earth and education: How America's commitment to equity will determine our future. *Educational Researcher, 36*(6), 318–334. doi:10.3102/0013189X07308253

Datnow, A., & Park, V. (2019). *Professional collaboration with purpose: Teacher learning towards equitable and excellent schools*. New York, NY: Routledge.

Davies, J., & Halsey, J. (2019). Principals as protagonists: Practices beneficent for indigenous education in rural schools. *Australian and International Journal of Rural Education, 29*(1), 101.

DeAngelis, C. A., Wolf, P. J., Maloney, L. D., & May, J. F. (2018). Charter school funding: (More) inequity in the city. *School Choice Demonstration Project*. Retrieved from https://scholarworks.uark.edu/scdp/1

Dearden, N. (2018, September 11). The UK must stop aid to failing private schools. *New Internationalist*. Retrieved from https://newint.org/features/2018/09/11/uk-must-stop-aid-failing-private-schools

DeLorenzo, R. A., & Battino, W. (2010). *Delivering on the promise: The education revolution*. Bloomington, IN: Solution Tree Press.

Desforges, C., & Abouchaar, A. (2003). *The impact of parental involvement, parental support and family education on pupil achievement and adjustment: A literature review* (Vol. 433). London, England: DfES.

Dobush, G. (2019, January 28). One country's solution to a teacher shortage: Cold, hard cash. *Fortune*. Retrieved from http://fortune.com/2019/01/28/england-teacher-shortages-cash-incentive/

DuFour, R. (2004). What is a "professional learning community"? *Educational Leadership, 61*(8), 6–11.

Dweck, C. (2015). Carol Dweck revisits the growth mindset. *Education Week, 35*(5), 20–24.

Edwards, S. (2018, February 9). Debate over for-profit schools in Uganda boils over as Bridge and others refuse to close. *Devex*. Retrieved from https://www.devex.com/news/debate-over-for-profit-schools-in-uganda-boils-over-as-bridge-and-others-refuse-to-close-92065

Evers, J., & Kneyber, R. (Eds.). (2015). *Flip the system: Changing education from the ground up*. New York, NY: Routledge.

Fallon, J. (2015, February 27). Pearson 2014 results. *Pearson.* Retrieved from https://www.pearson.com/corporate/news/media/news-announce ments/2015/02/pearson-2014-results.html

Financial Times. (n.d.). *Make informed decisions with the FT.* Retrieved from https://www.ft.com/content/c0b611fc-dab5-11e3-9a27-00144feabd c0?mhq5j=e7

Franklin, M. (2012, January 24). We risk losing education race, PM warns. *The Australian.*

Fullan, M. (Ed.). (2003). *The moral imperative of school leadership.* Thousand Oaks, CA: Corwin.

Fullan, M. (2009). Large-scale reform comes of age. *Journal of Educational Change, 10*(2/3), 101–113.

Fullan, M. (2011, April). *Choosing the wrong drivers for whole system reform.* CSE Seminar Series Paper 204, Centre for Strategic Education, Melbourne.

García, E., & Weiss, E. (2017, September 27). Education inequalities at the school starting gate. *Economic Policy Institute.* Retrieved from https://www .epi.org/publication/education-inequalities-at-the-school-starting-gate/

Global Accessibility News. (2017, August 10). *Children with disabilities struggle with schooling in South Korea.* Retrieved from http:// globalaccessibilitynews.com/2017/08/10/children-with-disabilities-struggle-with-schooling-in-south-korea/

Global Health Europe. (2009, August 24). *Inequity and inequality in health.* Retrieved from http://www.globalhealtheurope.org/index.php/resour ces/glossary/values/179-inequity-and-inequality-in-health.html

Goal 2. (n.d.). *End hunger, achieve food security and improve nutrition, and promote sustainable agriculture.* Retrieved from https://una-gp.org/clancyt/ files/goals/goal2.pdf

Goodall, J. (2017). *Narrowing the achievement gap: Parental/family engagement with children's learning.* New York, NY: Routledge.

Goodall, J. (2018a). A toolkit for parental/family engagement: From project to process. *School Leadership & Management, 38*(2), 222–238.

Goodall, J. (2018b). Engaging parents. *Learning Foundation.* Retrieved from https://learningfoundation.org.uk/5680-2/

Goodall, J. (2018c). Learning-centred parental/family engagement: Freire reimagined. *Educational Review, 70*(5), 603–621.

Goodall, J., & Weston, K. (2018, November 29). 100 ideas for primary teachers: Engaging parents. *Bloomsbury.* Retrieved from https:// www.bloomsbury.com/uk/100-ideas-for-primary-teachers-engaging-parents-9781472955180/

Grabmeier, J. A. (2019, April 4). A "million word gap" for children who aren't read to at home. *Ohio State News*. Retrieved from https://news.osu.edu/a-million-word-gap-for-children-who-arent-read-to-at-home/

Green, E. L. (2019, April 12). LeBron James opened a school that was considered an experiment. It's showing promise. *New York Times*. Retrieved from https://www.nytimes.com/2019/04/12/education/lebron-james-school-ohio.html

Hargreaves, A., & Dawe, R. (1990). Paths of professional development: Contrived collegiality, collaborative culture, and the case of peer coaching. *Teaching and Teacher Education, 6*(3), 227–241.

Hargreaves, A., & O'Connor, M. T. (2018). *Collaborative professionalism: When teaching together means learning for all.* Thousand Oaks, CA: Corwin.

Harris, A. (2008, January 7). Speaking at the International Conference of School Effectiveness and Improvement in New Zealand. (Also quoted in *The School Effectiveness Framework* by the Welsh Assembly Government.)

Harris, A. (2010). Improving schools in challenging contexts. In A. Hargreaves, A. Lieberman, M. Fullan, & D. Hopkins (Eds.), *Second international handbook of educational change* (pp. 693–706). Berlin, Germany: Springer, Dordrecht.

Harris, A. (2013). Distributed leadership: Friend or foe? *Educational Management Administration & Leadership, 41*(5), 545–554.

Harris, A., Andrew-Power, K., & Goodall, J. (2009). *Do parents know they matter? Raising achievement through parental engagement.* London, England: A&C Black.

Harris, A., & Goodall, J. (2008). Do parents know they matter? Engaging all parents in learning. *Educational Research, 50*(3), 277–289.

Harris, A., & Jones, M. (2010). Professional learning communities and system improvement. *Improving Schools, 13*(2), 172–181.

Harris, A., & Jones, M. (2015a). *Leading futures: Global perspectives on educational leadership.* Thousand Oaks, CA: SAGE.

Harris, A., & Jones, M. (2015b). Transforming education systems: Comparative and critical perspectives on school leadership. *Asia Pacific Journal of Education, 35*(1). doi:10.1080/02188791.2015.1056590

Harris, A., & Jones, M. (2017). Leading educational change and improvement at scale: Some inconvenient truths about system performance. *International Journal of Leadership in Education, 20*, 632–641.

Harris, A., Jones, M., & Huffman, J. (2017). *Teachers leading educational reform: The power and potential of professional learning communities.* New York, NY: Routledge.

Hattie, J. (2015). *The politics of distraction.* London, England: Pearson.

Holden, R., & Zhang, J. (n.d.). *The economic impact of improving regional, rural & remote education in Australia.* Sydney, NSW: Gonski Institute for Education. Retrieved from https://education.arts.unsw.edu.au/media/EDUCFile/Gonski_Institute_Report__Cost_of_Education_Gap.pdf

Holmes, E. (1911). *What is and what might be.* London, England: Constable and Co. Ltd.

Hopfenbeck, T., Lenkeit, J., Masri, Y., Cantrell, K., Ryan, J., & Baird, J. (2017). Lessons learned from PISA: A systematic review of peer-reviewed articles on the programme for international student assessment. *Scandinavian Journal of Educational Research, 62,* 333–353. doi:10.1080./00313831.2016.1258726

Human Rights Watch. (2013, July 15). *China: End discrimination, exclusion of children with disabilities.* Retrieved from https://www.hrw.org/news/2013/07/15/china-end-discrimination-exclusion-children-disabilities

Improving Teaching. (n.d.). *Characteristics of effective teacher professional development: What we know, what we don't, how we can find out.* Retrieved from https://improvingteaching.co.uk/characteristics-cpd/

Jensen, B. (2012, February 17). *Catching up: Learning from the best school systems in East Asia. Grattan Institute.* Retrieved from https://grattan.edu.au/report/catching-up-learning-from-the-best-school-systems-in-east-asia/

Jerrim, J. (2017, February). *Global gaps: Comparing socio-economic gaps in the performance of highly able UK pupils internationally.* Retrieved from https://www.suttontrust.com/wp-content/uploads/2017/02/Global-Gaps_FINAL_V2_WEB.pdf#page=6

Johansson, S. (2016). International large-scale assessments: What uses, what consequences? *Educational Research, 58,* 139–149.

Jones, M. S., Harris, A., Hooge, E., Doornenbal, J., Vermeulen, M., Wolff, R., . . . & Christians, J. (2017). *The Dutch way in education: Teach, learn and lead the Dutch way.* OMJS BV, Uitgeverij.

Joyce, B. R., & Showers, B. (1981). Transfer of training: The contribution of "coaching." *Journal of Education, 163*(2), 163–172.

Kawachi, I. (n.d.). *Faculty and researcher directory.* Boston, MA: Harvard T. H. Chan. Retrieved from https://www.hsph.harvard.edu/ichiro-kawachi/

Kerr, K., & Ainscow, M. (2017). *Equity in education: Time to stop and think. A report on the state of equity in the English education system.* Manchester, England: The University of Manchester.

Kopp, W. (2012, May 13). In defense of optimism in education. *HuffPost.* Retrieved from https://www.huffpost.com/entry/in-defense-of-optimism-in_b_1338763?guccounter=1&guce_referrer=aHR0cHM6Ly93d3cuZ29vZ2xlLmNvbS8&guce_referrer_sig=AQAAAKAgcuRFgzPufMhCTL_kRrih

QR5PB2d qyB7iqWeQnay_Gd-klSxpLxECY480M5dFrGLQNf3Pj-ksrStoZ
aajWdRLH5LfaDUydqnoiGB0vzAnVf2jXjM463dWTPhjA4tyyCaSGl3eP
xJC2wkGQrx89BtFRNKbjMo6f7_G7a3JUwV2

Kyriakides, L., Georgiou, M. P., Creemers, B. P. M., Panayiotou, A., & Reynolds, D. (2018). The impact of national educational policies on student achievement: A European study. *School Effectiveness and School Improvement, 29*(2), 171–203.

Leithwood, K., Harris, A., & Hopkins, D. (2008). Seven strong claims about successful school leadership. *School Leadership and Management, 28*(1), 27–42.

Leithwood, K., Harris, A., & Strauss, T. (2010). *Leading school turnaround: How successful leaders transform low-performing schools.* Hoboken, NJ: John Wiley & Sons.

Lepkowska, D., & Nightingale, J. (2019). *Meet the parents: How schools can work effectively with families to support children's learning.* New York, NY: Routledge.

Liang, X., Kidwai, H., & Zhang, M. (2016). How Shanghai does it: Insights and lessons from the highest-ranking education system in the world. *The World Bank.* Retrieved from http://www.worldbank.org/en/topic/ education/publication/how-shanghai-does-it

Liu, Y. (2016). *Higher education, meritocracy and inequality in China.* The Netherlands: Springer Press.

Mann, H. (1848). *Twelfth Annual Report to the Secretary of the Massachusetts State Board of Education.* Retrieved from https://genius.com/Horace-mann-twelfth-annual-report-to-the-secretary-of-the-massachusetts-state-board-of-education-1848-annotated

Martin, W. (2015, October 16). This tutor in Hong Kong is so good he was offered a job worth $11 million, but he said no. *Business Insider.* Retrieved from http://uk.businessinsider.com/hong-kong-tutors-can-make-millions-of-dollars-2015-10

Mental Health Foundation. (n.d.). *Children and young people.* Retrieved from https://www.mentalhealth.org.uk/a-to-z/c/children-and-young-people

Meyers, C. V., & Darwin, M. J. (Eds.). (2017). *Enduring myths that inhibit school turnaround.* Charlotte, NC: Information Age Publishing.

Meyers, C. V., & Smylie, M. A. (2017). Five myths of school turnaround policy and practice. *Leadership and Policy in Schools, 16*(3), 502–523.

Morgan, N. S. (2016). *Engaging families in schools: Practical strategies to improve parental involvement.* New York, NY: Routledge.

Netolicky, D. M., Andrews, J., & Paterson, C. (Eds.). (2018). *Flip the system Australia: What matters in education.* New York, NY: Routledge.

Organization for Economic Cooperation and Development (OECD). (2013). *PISA 2012 results: What makes schools successful, resources, policies and practice* (Vol. IV). Paris, France: Author. Retrieved from www.oecd.org/pisa/keyfindings/pisa-results

Organization for Economic Cooperation and Development (OECD). (2018, May 29). *World class: How to build a 21st-century school system*. Retrieved from http://www.oecd.org/education/world-class-9789264300002-en.htm

Parliament of Australia. (n.d.). *Executive summary*. Retrieved from https://www.aph.gov.au/parliamentary_business/committees/senate/school_funding/school_funding/report/a03

Patrinos, H. (2011, August 9). Can the private sector play a helpful role in education? *The Guardian*. Retrieved from http://www.theguardian.com/education/mortarboard/2011/aug/09/private-sector-role-in-education

Pearson. (2014, December 10). *Pearson to develop PISA 2018 Student Assessment 21st Century Frameworks for OECD*. Retrieved from https://www.pearson.com/corporate/news/media/news-announcements/2014/12/pearson-to-develop-pisa-2018-student-assessment-21st-century-fra.html

Polianskaya, A. (2018, July 1). Education reforms causing greater inequality in schools, major study finds. *Independent*. Retrieved from https://www.independent.co.uk/news/education/education-news/coalition-education-reforms-inequality-schools-study-government-criticism-a8425686.html

Pollock, M. (2017). *Schooltalk: Rethinking what we say about and to students every day*. New York, NY: The New Press.

Qin, A. (2017, August 5). Britain turns to Chinese textbooks to improve its math scores. *New York Times*. Retrieved from https://www.nytimes.com/2017/08/05/world/asia/china-textbooks-britain.html

Ravitch, D. (2000). *Left behind: A century of failed school reforms*. New York, NY: Simon.

Ravitch, D. (2016). *The death and life of the great American school system: How testing and choice are undermining education*. New York, NY: Basic Books.

Ravitch, D. (2020). *Slaying Goliath: The passionate resistance to privatization and the fight to save America's public schools*. New York, NY: Knopf.

Rayner, J. (2012, September 15). School budget cuts spell hunger for many pupils as breakfast clubs close. *The Guardian*. Retrieved from https://www.theguardian.com/education/2012/sep/16/school-budget-cuts-breakfast-clubs

Richardson, H. (2019, April 16). Four out of 10 teachers plan to quit, survey suggests. *BBC News*. Retrieved from https://www.bbc.co.uk/news/education-47936211

Roberts, J. (2018, July 20). Exclusive: England "wrong to copy Shanghai maths." *tes*. Retrieved from https://www.tes.com/news/exclusive-england-wrong-copy-shanghai-maths

Roberts, J. (2019, April 12). Exclusive: "Zero-tolerance" academy softens its punishments. *tes*. Retrieved from https://www.tes.com/news/exclusive-zero-tolerance-academy-softens-its-punishments

Robinson, M. (2019, March 18). It's time to talk about charter school privilege. *The Progressive*. Retrieved from https://progressive.org/public-school-shakedown/its-time-to-talk-about-charter-school-privilege-robinson-190318/

Robinson, V. (2017). *Reduce change to increase improvement*. Thousand Oaks, CA: Corwin.

Rolfe, H. (2015). No quick fix for pupils with a fixed mindset about their own intelligence. *The Conversation*. Retrieved from https://theconversation.com/no-quick-fix-for-pupils-with-a-fixed-mindset-about-their-own-intelligence-43152

Sahlberg, P. (2018). *Equitable education in Australia. Flip the system Australia: What matters in education*. New York, NY: Routledge.

Sahlberg, P., & Hasak, J. (2016). "Big data" was supposed to fix education. It didn't. It's time for "small data." *The Washington Post*. Retrieved from www.washingtonpost.com/news/answer-sheet/wp/2016/05/09/big-data-was-supposed-to-fix-education-it-didnt-its-time-for-small-data/

Scottish Government. (2018, September 13). *Attainment Scotland fund: Local authority mini survey analysis—summer 2018*. Retrieved from https://www.gov.scot/publications/evaluation-attainment-scotland-fund-analysis-local-authority-mini-survey-summer/pages/3/

Sharratt, L. (2018). *Clarity: What matters most in learning, teaching, and leading*. Thousand Oaks, CA: Corwin.

Sharratt, L., & Planche, B. (2016). *Leading collaborative learning: Empowering excellence*. Thousand Oaks, CA: Corwin.

Shirley, D. (2016). *The new imperatives of educational change: Achievement with integrity*. New York, NY: Routledge.

Shirley, D. (2017). Review of global education reform: How privatization and public investment influence education outcomes. *Education Review/Reseñas Educativas*, 24.

Sims, S., & Fletcher-Wood, H. (2018). *Characteristics of effective teacher professional development: What we know, what we don't, how we can find out*. Retrieved from https://www.teachertoolkit.co.uk/wp-content/uploads/2018/10/Characteristics-of-Effective-Teacher-Professional-Development.pdf

Sjöberg, S. (2019). The PISA-syndrome—How the OECD has hijacked the way we perceive pupils, schools and education. *Confero: Essays on Education, Philosophy and Politics*, 7(1), 12–65.

Sustainable Development Goals. (2015). *Goal 4.1*. Retrieved from http://indicators.report/targets/4-1/

Tai, J. (2016, May 31). Singaporeans "don't walk the talk" on special needs kids. *The Straits Times*. Retrieved from https://www.straitstimes.com/singapore/sporeans-dont-walk-the-talk-on-special-needs-kids

Timperley, H., Wilson, A., Barrar, H., & Fung, I. (2007). *Teacher professional learning and development: Best evidence synthesis iteration*. Wellington, New Zealand: Ministry of Education.

Transparency International. (2013). *Global corruption report: Education*. New York, NY: Routledge. Retrieved from https://web.edu.hku.hk/f/acadstaff/376/Global%20Corruption%20Report%3A%20Education.pdf

United Nations Children's Fund (UNICEF). (2018). *An unfair start: Inequality in children's education in rich countries* (Innocenti Report Card No. 15).

United Nations Educational, Scientific, and Cultural Organization (UNESCO). (n.d.). *Indonesia*. Retrieved from https://www.education-inequalities.org/countries/indonesia#?dimension=all&group=all&year=latest

Vescio, V., Ross, D., & Adams, A. (2008). A review of research on the impact of professional learning communities on teaching practice and student learning. *Teaching and Teacher Education*, *24*(1), 80–91.

Weale, S. (2018a, January 25). One in eight secondary schools in England are "failing." *The Guardian*. Retrieved from https://www.theguardian.com/education/2018/jan/25/one-in-eight-secondary-schools-in-england-are-failing-dfe-data-shows

Weale, S. (2018b, May 17). Stress and serious anxiety: How the new GCSE is affecting mental health. *The Guardian*. Retrieved from https://www.theguardian.com/education/2018/may/17/stress-and-serious-anxiety-how-the-new-gcse-is-affecting-mental-health

Whitty, G., & Anders, J. (2017). "Closing the achievement gap" in English cities and towns in the twenty-first century. In W. Pink & G. Noblit (Eds.), *Second international handbook of urban education* (pp. 1079–1101). Cham, Switzerland: Springer International Handbooks of Education.

Wingfield, A. H. (2019, April 3). Abandoning public education will be considered unthinkable 50 years from now. *Vox*. Retrieved from https://www.vox.com/2019/3/27/18226303/public-private-school-choice

Woo, W. T. (2019, March 27). Decentralising Malaysia's education system. *East Asia Forum*. Retrieved from https://www.eastasiaforum.org/2019/03/27/decentralising-malaysias-education-system/

World Bank. (2009). *The role and impact of public–private partnership*. Retrieved from http://siteresources.worldbank.org/EDUCATION/Resources

World Health Organization. (2017). *10 facts on health inequities and their causes.* Retrieved from https://www.who.int/features/factfiles/health_inequities/en/

Yang, C. (2016, May 23). Super tutors who earn at least $1m a year. *The Straits Times.* Retrieved from http://www.straitstimes.com/singapore/super-tutors-who-earn-at-least-1m-a-year

Yorke, H. (2017). *More than 20,000 university students buying essays and dissertations as Lords call for ban on "contract cheating."* Retrieved from https://www.telegraph.co.uk/education/2017/01/13/20000-university-students-buying-essays-dissertations-lords/

Zhao, Y. (2016). From deficiency to strength: Shifting the mindset about education inequality. *Journal of Social Issues, 72*(4), 716–735.

Zhao, Y. (2017). What works may hurt: Side effects in education. *Journal of Educational Change, 18*(1), 1–19.

Zhao, Y. (2018). *Reach for greatness: Personalizable education for all children.* Thousand Oaks, CA: Corwin.

Zhao, Y. (2018). *What works may hurt: Side effects in education.* New York, NY: Teachers College Press.

Zhao, Y. (2019). Side effects in education: Winners and losers in school voucher programs. *Phi Delta Kappan, 100*(5), 63–66.

Index

Page references followed by (figure) indicate an illustrated figure.

Economic Policy Institute, 18
Education
    as important global currency, 1
    social and income mobility
        through, 18
    UN conventions on universal
        right to equal, 10–11
    See also Student performance
Education Endowment
    Foundation (EEF) [UK], 2
Education equity
    Finland, the Netherlands, and
        Canada's efforts toward,
        15–16, 17
    important of committing entire
        system to, 16
    OECD's increased focus on, 39
    Pollock's definition of, 21
    problem of emphasizing
        excellence over, 23–25
    by providing equal
        opportunities, 22
    recalibrating policies toward, 19
    school choice eroding, 24, 27
    system change to increase,
        39–41
    See also Education inequity;
        Leading for equity
Education hard truths
    1: privatization and private
        sector intervention, 49–51
    2: context and culture matter,
        51–54
    3: inequality, 54–57
    4: politics and corruption,
        57–59
    See also Student performance
Education inequalities
    continuing in developed and
        developing countries, 11
    research findings on effects
        of, 17
    resource redistribution to
        correct, 12–13
    See also Inequalities
Education inequity
    as greatest educational
        challenge, 1, 2
    how it disenfranchise students,
        16–17

    macro influences on, 6–7,
        49–59, 104
    micro influences on, 6–7, 63–76,
        78–85, 93
    radical rethinking required to
        solve, 4–5
    report (2018) on English
        education reforms causing,
        9–10
    as root cause of educational
        failure, 61
    See also Education equity;
        Inequity
Education policies
    accountability and privatization
        focus of, 34
    emphasizing excellence over
        equity problem of, 23–25
    insufficiency of token, 18
    moving away from the OECD
        vision of excellence, 108
    time to consider the best,
        18–19
    understanding there are no
        simple solutions, 106–107
    unintended consequences of,
        22–23
    within-system learning applied
        to, 107–109
Education Policy Institute report
    (2017), 46
Education reform
    disruptive process and
        emotional costs of, 33–35
    improved performance is
        possible from, 38
    market-led, 50–51
    recalibrating toward equity, 19
    what is required for true,
        105–109
    the *wrong drivers* for, 34–35
    See also Educational
        interventions; Macro
        influences; Micro
        influences
Education reform framework
    1: borrow design principles
        instead of policies, 59–60
    2: focus on countries that are
        similar, 60

Grattan Institute report (Australia), 25, 31
Great Britain. *See* United Kingdom (UK)

"Hard to reach" parents, 80
Hargreaves, A., 96
Harvard University, 9
Hasak, J., 49
Hattie, J., 95
Health
social inequalities related to poor, 2, 9
socioeconomic status linked to, 1
High-stake testing accountability
harm of the relentless pursuit of, 25
New York State's abandonment of computer-based, 27
as possible reform area, 107
See also PISA (Program for International Student Assessment)
Higher School Certificate (HSC) [Australia], 13
Hofstede's Power Distance Index (PDI), 54–56
Holmes, Edmond, 103
Hong Kong schools, 32, 43, 52, 54, 56
Hub schools (UK), 51–52
Human capital gap, 106

Income differences
growing wealth divide, 17
private tutoring access and, 56–57
problem of inequalities in, 2–4, 9
providing comparative advantage for student, 43–44, 56–57
social inequities as disparities in, 10
as student performance factor, 54–57
See also Poverty
Indonesia, 35, 36 (figure), 44, 50, 53, 54

Inequalities
as being a social failure, 104
cultural differences in perceived, 54–56
differentiating between inequity and, 10
how they impact student performance, 54–57
international discourse on, 18
power Distance Index (PDI), 54–56
of private tutoring access, 56–57
problem of health, income, and social, 2–4, 9
research findings on effects of, 17
See also Education inequalities
Inequity
as being an injustice, 10
challenge of dismantling structural, 14
differentiating between inequality and, 10
how education systems contribute to, 5
international discourse on, 18
See also Education inequity; Poverty
Integrating strategies and approaches, 72 (figure), 73

Joyce, B. R., 96

Kawachi, Ichiro, 9
Kerr, Kirsten, 19, 103
Ketuanan Melayu (Malay supremacy) [Malaysia], 57
Khamarov, Eli, 63
Kopp, Wendy, 1

Language differences
as barrier to parental/family engagement, 80
education inequities due to, 52–54
parental engagement impact on students with, 89
Leading for equity
benefits of, 75–76
in Cabramatta High School, 66–67

National Assessment Program—
Literacy and Numeracy
(NAPLAN) [Australia],
14, 24–25
National Education Union
(NEU), 105
The Netherlands, 15
Non-English-speaking background
(NESB) students, 52–54, 80, 89

OECD (Organization for
Economic Cooperation and
Development)
education excellence vision
of the, 26, 108
Frameworks for PISA 2018
awarded to Pearson by,
26–27
increased focus on education
equity by, 39
OECD report (2018) on
educational inequality and
inequity, 17
PISA data use promoted by,
28–29
"resiliency" argument of, 39, 54
*World Class: Building a 21st
Century School System* report
(2018), 38
OECD countries
average higher education
attainment in, 16
expenditures on public and
private institutions in, 50
participating in PISA, 35–39
See also Developed countries
Opportunities
education equity to provide
students equal, 22
understanding that context
impacts access to, 46–47
See also Leading for equity
"Out of school" children data,
44–45

Parental/family engagement
barriers to, 82–85
building a learning community
with, 93
building education equity by, 69

rationale for, 78
what we know about student
learning and, 79–80
See also Communities
Parental/family involvement
engagement vs., 79
student achievement and, 81–82
Parents/families
educational attitudes and
behaviors of, 81
engagement vs. involvement of,
79, 81–82
"hard to reach," 80
why they matter to education
equity, 8082
Pearson, 27, 50, 51
Peru, 36 (figure), 38
Philippines, 36 (figure), 44, 50, 54, 56
Piccoli, Adrian, 103
PISA (Program for International
Student Assessment)
"Baby PISA" testing, 26
comparison of country rankings
on, 19–20, 28–29, 30–31,
32–33, 38, 41
countries opting out of, 27–28
excellence versus equity
problem and limitations of,
25, 27–31, 33
Frameworks for PISA 2018 to be
developed by Pearson, 26–27
OECD countries participating
in, 35–39
OECD's promotion of, 28–29
as possible reform area, 107
See also Accountability;
High-stake testing
accountability; Learning
assessment
PISA Top 10, 30
Plutarch, 9
Politics and corruption, 57–59
Pollock, Mica, 21
Positive reinforcement, 68
Poverty
educational inequity linked to,
44–46, 54–57
global and regional trends
in extreme (1981–2005),
3 (figure)

Schooltalk (Pollock), 21
Scottish Government's Pupil
  Equity Funding in, 12
Shanghai schools, 31, 32, 37, 40,
  52, 107
Shower, B., 96
Singapore
  English proficiency of students
    in, 53
  gross national income per
    capital in, 37
  high math performance of
    students in, 52
  income and private
    tutoring advantage of
    students in, 43–44,
    56–57
  PISA ranking of, 36 (figure)
  schools in, 20–21, 28
  special needs students in,
    20–21, 38
Social inequalities
  differentiating between
    inequities and, 10
  educational inequity linked to,
    44–46
  poor health related to income
    and, 1–2, 9
  Power Distance Index (PDI)
    indicator of, 54–56
Social inequities
  description of, 10
  differentiating between
    inequalities and, 10
Social mobility, 18
Socioeconomic status
  health status linked to, 1
  as predictor of student
    performance, 18
South Asian "mastery" teaching
  approach, 51–52
South Korea
  income advantage of students
    in, 43–44, 54
  special needs students in,
    20, 38
Special needs students
  hurdles for Chinese, 20
  Singaporean, Chinese, South
    Korean, 20–21, 38

Standardization
  any gain as starting to
    plateau, 85
  findings on damage caused by,
    23, 34–35
  Global Education Reform
    Movement (GERM)
    emphasis on, 30
Stringfield, Sam, 109
Student performance
  challenges of finding real
    explanations for, 49
  geographic area as predictor
    of, 17
  Grattan Institute report
    on mental illness and
    pressures for, 25
  personal and social costs of
    underachievement, 4
  "resiliency" linked to higher,
    39, 54
  social class as predictor
    of, 18
  societal and systemic causes of
    poor, 2, 4
  See also Education; Education
    hard truths
Students
  benefits of positive
    reinforcement for, 68
  cycle of underachievement by
    disadvantaged, 86
  engaging parents and families
    of, 69, 77–91
  how educational inequity
    disenfranchises, 16–17
  non-English-speaking
    background, 52–54,
    80, 89
  providing equal opportunities
    to, 22
  providing mindset training
    to, 2
  special needs, 20–21, 38
  See also Learning
Sustainability Development Goals
  (2015–2030), 11, 43
Sutton Trust, 12
Sweden, 56
The Sydney Morning Herald, 31

Teacher shortage, 34
Teachers
building professional learning
community of, 69–70
comparing experience in
developed and developing
countries, 37
"contrived collegiality"
between, 96
education reform challenges for,
33–34
growing disillusionment and
shortage of, 34
need for interagency work to
support, 46
positive reinforcement by, 68
professional development
support of Shanghai's, 40
strike (2018) by West Virginian,
50–51
Teaching
leading for equity focus on, 68
UK's hub schools using South
Asian "mastery" approach
for, 51–52
Technical and Further Education
(TAFE) [Australia], 89
Text book publishing corruption,
58–59
Thailand, 37
Turkey, 35

United Kingdom (UK)
Education Policy Institute report
(2017) on schools in, 46
educational inequity in, 9–10
Power Distance Index (PDI)
score of, 56
South Asian "mastery" teaching
approach in hub schools
of, 51–52
United Nations
Convention on the Rights of
the Child, 10–11
global institutions reinforcing
educational ideas of, 30

Millennium Development
Goals, 11
Sustainability Development
Goals (2015–2030),
11, 43
UN Educational, Scientific, and
Cultural Organization
(UNESCO), 10, 30
Universal Declaration of Human
Rights (1948), 10
United States
college admissions scandal
in, 44
experience of teachers in, 37
PISA ranking of, 36 (figure)
Power Distance Index (PDI)
score of, 56
University of South Wales,
103, 106
University of Southern
California, 44

Vietnam, 37

"We Risk Losing Education Race,
PM Warns" (*The Australian*),
30–31
Wealth divide, 17
West Virginia teacher strike (2018),
50–51
Wheelers online library, 13
Whole-school professional learning
communities (PLCs), 97
Within-school professional learning
communities (PLCs), 97
Within-system learning,
107–109
Wolf, P. J., 47
World Bank, 30, 51
World Bank report (2016), 40
*World Class: Building a 21st Century
School System* report (OECD,
2018), 38
World-class education fallacy, 38

Zhao, Yong, 22, 52

A SAGE Publishing Company

Helping educators make the greatest impact

CORWIN HAS ONE MISSION: to enhance education through intentional professional learning.

We build long-term relationships with our authors, educators, clients, and associations who partner with us to develop and continuously improve the best evidence-based practices that establish and support lifelong learning.

Leadership That Makes an Impact

LYN SHARRATT

Explore 14 essential parameters to guide system and school leaders toward building powerful collaborative learning cultures.

MICHAEL FULLAN

How do you break the cycle of surface-level change to tackle complex challenges? *Nuance* is the answer.

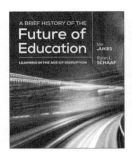

IAN JUKES & RYAN L. SCHAAF

The digital environment has radically changed how students need to learn. Get ready to be challenged to accommodate today's learners.

JOANNE MCEACHEN & MATTHEW KANE

Getting at the heart of what matters for students is key to deeper learning that connects with their lives.

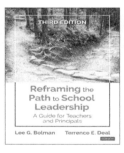

LEE G. BOLMAN & TERRENCE E. DEAL

Sometimes all it takes to solve a problem is to reframe it by listening to wise advice from a trusted mentor.

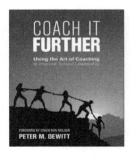

PETER M. DEWITT

This go-to guide is written for coaches, leaders looking to be coached, and leaders interested in coaching burgeoning leaders.

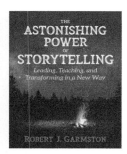

ROBERT J. GARMSTON
Stories have unique power to captivate and motivate action. This guidebook shows how to leverage storytelling to engage students.

JOYCE L. EPSTEIN
Strengthen programs of family and community engagement to promote equity and increase student success!

MICHAEL FULLAN, JOANNE QUINN, & JOANNE MCEACHEN,
This book defines what deep learning is, and takes up the question of how to mobilize complex whole-system change.

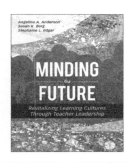

ANGELINE A. ANDERSON, SUSAN K. BORG, & STEPHANIE L. EDGAR
Centered on teacher voice and grounded in foundations of collaboration and data-informed planning, Transform Academy comes to life through its stories, and accompanying action steps.

AMY TEPPER & PATRICK FLYNN
Leaders know that feedback is essential to teacher development. This how-to guide helps leaders conduct comprehensive observations, analyze lessons, develop high-leverage action steps, and craft effective feedback.

JOANNE QUINN, JOANNE MCEACHEN, MICHAEL FULLAN, MAG GARDNER, & MAX DRUMMY
This resource shows you how to design deep learning, measure progress, and assess the conditions to sustain innovation and mobilization.